A
SHORT
AND
REMARKABLE
HISTORY
OF
NEW YORK
CITY

A
SHORT
AND
REMARKABLE
HISTORY
OF

New York City

Jane Mushabac
and
Angela Wigan

With
illustrations from
the Museum of the
City of New York

FORDHAM
UNIVERSITY
PRESS

New York
1999

To the historians of New York City,

    past and present

To our families—

    Arthur, Ben, Dan, and David;

    Mel and Kate

Copyright © 1999
by Jane Mushabac and Angela Wigan

Library of Congress Cataloging-in-Publication Data
Mushabac, Jane.
    A short and remarkable history of New York City /
Jane Mushabac and Angela Wigan : with illustrations
from the Museum of the City of New York.
    p. cm.
   Includes bibliographical references and index.
   ISBN 0-8232-1984-4 — ISBN 0-8232-1985-2 (pbk.)
    1. New York (N.Y.)—History—Chronology. 2.
New York (N.Y.)—History—Pictorial works. I. Title:
New York City. II. Wigan, Angela. III. Museum of
the City of New York. IV. Title.
F128.3.M945   1999
974.7′1′00202—dc21
                          99-046888

Design by Omega Clay
The 2002 printing corrected minor errors and includes
the events of September 11, 2001.

Fourth printing 2006.

Seal of the
Province of
New Netherland,
1623

Contents

Seal of the
City of New
Amsterdam,
1654

Seal of
New York City,
1915

Current Seal of
New York City

INTRODUCTION

New Yorkers love to watch the building of a new skyscraper—particularly the digging of a foundation—through small holes cut into a wooden construction fence. It's one of the great lunch-hour pastimes. Over the years the ubiquitous observer has watched the City grow and change—sometimes with disapproval, sometimes with elation, always with a fond curiosity.

This short book, with its events and anecdotes, is a peephole for spying on the history of the City from its foundations up to the present. New York was always destined to be a place of migrants and immigrants. People have come to this mercantile center to work, to build, to learn, to play, and to settle down in a neighborhood. Its people give the City the energy that makes living here a heightened experience.

The following timeline of five hundred years of New York City history can be read as a story, used for reference, or browsed through for fun.

Indians are here first . . .

By 1500, Lenapes ("the People") have lived in the area of Greater New York City for 1,500 years. They call their homeland Lenapehoking. Earlier native people roamed the vast forests and coastal plains for ten thousand years to hunt, gather, and fish.

Cultivation has brought the Lenapes a more settled way of life. Among their bands are Canarsee, Rockaway, Wiechquaesgeck, Manhattan, Hackensack, and Rechgawawank Indians. Until the late 1600s a Rechgawawank planting ground was in use in Inwood on Manhattan Island. A ceremonial rock shelter can still be seen there.

The Indians' main highways are the waters along the 770-mile coastline of New York Harbor. Indian trails follow the high ground to avoid marshes and swamps; they are in use today as our Broadway, Flatbush Avenue, and Kings Highway.

The Hackensack Indians paddle across the great river to Sapokanikan, now the West Village, to trade and to plant corn and tobacco. Manhattan Island is a central trading place for goods and ideas.

Spirituality governs all Lenape life. The Creator, Kishelemukong, creates people by his thoughts. Everything in nature is alive and possesses a spirit, or *manetu*. Spirits watch over the four quarters of the world.

A creation myth says this world is built on the back of a giant turtle. A small petroglyph of a turtle, made by Lenapes and found near the Bronx River, is on display at the New York Botanical Garden.

Land is the gift of the Creator.

Turtle petroglyph carved by Lenape Indians

Longhouses as drawn by a European artist

Lenapes live by the seasons. In spring they plant tobacco, melons, and the three sisters, corn, beans, and squash. The great runs of shad up the rivers in May draw them to their summer campgrounds. Deer and migrating waterfowl are hunted in the autumn by groups using traps, fire-surround methods, or bow and arrow. Beaver trapping in winter provides furs at their thickest. People take shelter in longhouses, their fire-lit multiple-family dwellings. In the dark cold they make objects for trade, repair their weapons made of stone, wood, sinew, and bone, and tell lesson-stories to their children.

Lenape Indians of this area are respected for their independence. They are seen as ancestral by newer migrants from the south, and stand their ground against warrior groups from harsher climates to the north. Unlike the Iroquois, Lenapes live in unfortified villages. A fierce rigor in self-defense keeps other Indians away.

Lenape society is matrilineal: power is passed down through the female line. Both women and men can be leaders (sachems), first among equals. Women are often the peacemakers with a voice in council, but are never the only emissaries for treaties.

Women own the longhouses and contents, as well as the crops in the fields. A man marries into the woman's clan and village. Women and men share the labor, but their jobs are clearly defined. Women stay close to home; men roam farther afield to hunt and trade.

Children are much prized as long as there is enough food.

The few older people of forty or more are honored and regarded as favored. They are often herbalists, healers, and preservers of legend and song.

Burial is in shallow graves lined with bark or skins. The body, dressed in new clothes for the journey to the Creator, is folded, knees drawn up and arms across the chest. Gifts are placed with the body for use in the afterlife.

The Starry Path, our Milky Way, guides the souls of the dead on their journey. Each star represents the footprint of a traveling soul.

Lenapes speak Munsee (now Delaware), a dialect belonging to the Algonquian language group, described as sounding "sweet and full of meaning."

Kwĕlaha apchìch wémi awèn mwĕshalawoo yuk Lĕnapeyok (Let us hope that the Lenape will be remembered forever), says Lucy Parks Blalock, speaker of the Delaware language.

In 1500, five thousand Lenapes are the only people living in what is now New York City. By 1700, wars, epidemics, and displacement by European settlers reduce the Lenapes to two hundred.

Europeans arrive...

During the 1500s, French, Spanish, English, and Dutch sailors visit the area for fishing and trading.

Explorers are an international breed and work for whoever will pay. The French and Spanish each discover New York Harbor, but are too busy carving up Europe and the New World to imagine that New York is going to be one of the greatest cities in the world.

1524 The great sails of Giovanni da Verrazano's caravel *Dauphine* appear in New York Bay. The Florentine navigator, exploring for the King of France, is the first known European to sight and describe the Hudson River and the surrounding land.

1524 Verrazano, out in the bay in a small boat, is driven back to his ship by a sudden storm and leaves the land he has just discovered with "much regret, because of its commodiousness and beauty." Four centuries later the bridge that spans the narrow strait at the mouth of New York Harbor is named for him.

1525 Esteban Gómez, a black Portuguese explorer sailing for the Spanish, enters the Hudson River. He catches sight of tall, vigorous native people who are great archers.

1598 Dutch sea traders from Greenland sail south to winter on Manhattan. French hunters trap beavers in the neighborhood.

Giovanni da Verrazano

1600s Overcrowded Europe suffers from plagues and wars. Religious refugees from many countries take sanctuary in the Netherlands and become explorers and entrepreneurs. The Dutch, urban and resourceful, will give New York City its European beginnings.

1602 Rich from buying and selling, the Dutch in Europe establish the first of their great monopolies, the Dutch East India Company, and grab the lucrative trade of the Spice Islands.

1606 The English Crown loudly claims virtually all of North America. The claim is based on the legendary twelfth-century expedition of the Welsh explorer Madoc ap Owen Gwyneth, as well as the voyage of John Cabot to North America in 1497.

Henry Hudson

THE HALF-MOON.

Lenapes are called *peau rouge* or redskin because they decorate their bodies and faces with red ochre or dye taken from bloodroot.

1609 To keep their edge in trade, the Dutch hire away the English explorer Henry Hudson, whose route brings him to New York Bay in the eighty-ton *Half Moon*. He anchors off Manhattan's shore, and twenty-eight canoes with Lenape men, women, and children paddle out to greet him.

1609 For ten days Hudson sails up the river to be named for him until he reaches the "end of the Rivers Navigablenesse" near what is now Albany. His boatswain's mate, John Coleman, is killed by an arrow during an expedition. Because of misunderstandings and fear, ten Indians are killed with swords and guns by the crew.

1609 On his homeward journey, Hudson ends up in England and his maps are confiscated by the English, who are still angry at him for exploring for the Dutch.

1609 The beaver pelts Hudson takes home, which he bought from the Indians for beads, knives, and hatchets, are just as fine as the Russian skins that Europeans have to pay for in gold.

The Lenapes welcome the opportunity to trade with Europeans, whose goods bring ease from the labor of everyday survival. They are eager to share their food, furs, and expertise in exchange for metal axes and kettles, duffel cloth and beads.

1613 The Dutch fur merchant Adriaen Block sails around Manhattan, establishing that it's an island, but his ship, the *Tyger*, burns and sinks. Centuries later its timbers are in the collections of the Museum of the City of New York.

1613 Lenapes feed the *Tyger*'s stranded crew all winter and share their know-how with them. The crew build a new sixteen-ton ship, *Onrust*, which Block sails up the East River in 1614, through turbulent Hell Gate to what is now Block Island.

1613 In their European ships moored in the harbor, the "Salty People" squabble over furs and trade.

1614 Block and twelve other merchants decide cooperation is better than cutthroat competition and together form the short-lived New Netherland Company to cash in on New World fishing and fur trading.

1614 Europeans see simply dressed, healthy-looking people who wear fur cloaks in winter, or capes studded with turkey feathers, over their deerskin breechcloths or wrap skirts. Men do not wear feather headdresses; they sometimes shave their heads except for a ridge from brow to neck, or a scalplock.

Tea made from milkweed root is used by Indian people to treat diarrhea and fever. Many other flowers and plants which grow in the City parks today had medicinal uses for the Lenapes.

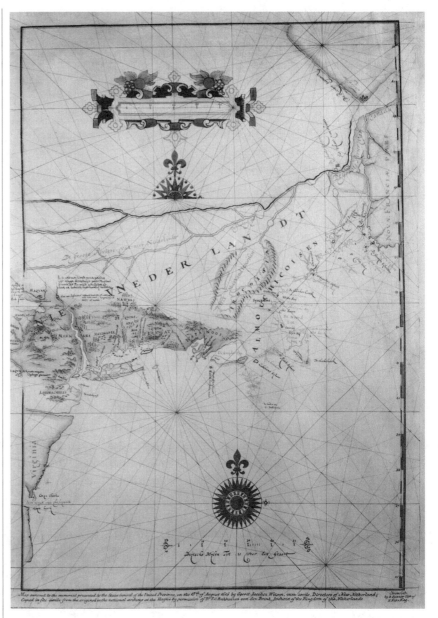

Block's Figurative Map of New Netherland

1621 Trading and empire-building get serious. The new Dutch West India Company, modeled on the Dutch East India Company, is granted a twenty-four-year charter by the Dutch government. For a time these two great corporations are the richest in the world.

1623 Aware of the value of colonists, the Dutch accept a petition for New World settlement by a group of Walloons, French-speaking Protestant refugees. These non-Dutch people have the opening role in the official Dutch history of New York City.

Flag of the West India Company

The Dutch put down stakes . . .

1624 The 260-ton *Nieu Nederlandt* brings thirty families, mostly Walloons, to New Netherland. Eight men settle on Nut Island, now Governors Island. The rest of the group stakes out New Netherland's northern boundaries up the Hudson River and in Connecticut, and its southern boundary in Delaware.

1624 In the company's first year of trade, 4,000 beaver pelts and 700 otter skins are shipped out of New Netherland. Across the ocean in Europe the pelts make luxurious cloaks and the wildly popular beaver hat.

1625 To stock the settlement once and for all, an expedition arrives with an engineer and more colonists, horses, sheep, hogs, cows, blacksmithing and farming tools, cloth, flour, firearms, and a ton of items to be used as trade goods.

The voyage from Europe can be made in as little as seven weeks. The ships sail down the west coast of Africa to the Canary Islands, then across the Atlantic with the trade winds in only fourteen days, and up the east coast of America.

Manhattan, the Lenape word for island, is spelled fifty different ways in early Dutch, French, and English records, from "Menatay" to "Manahata" to "Manatoes."

"The air in the New Netherlands is so dry, sweet and healthy . . . there are no heavy damps or stinking mists in the country." —Adriaen Van der Donck

1625 Brooklyn's first European settlers build a few huts on the shore of Wallabout Bay.

1625 Four stockholders of the Dutch West India Company send out their own trading ship from Amsterdam, ignoring their company's fur trade monopoly. The underground economy begins.

1625 The company instructs its men to find unoccupied land or talk the *wilden* (the native people) into agreeing to give up their land, "without however forcing them thereto in the least or taking possession by craft or fraud, lest we call down the wrath of God upon our unrighteous beginnings."

1626 The Dutch trade sixty guilders' worth of goods for Manhattan Island in a land deal with Lenapes, who use the island for hunting and trade. To the Europeans this deal is final; the Lenapes intend to share the land for a season or so.

1626   Construction of Fort Amsterdam begins at the southern tip of Manhattan.

1626   Colonists are scattered around New Netherland, vulnerable to attack and hard-pressed for survival. Director-general Peter Minuit orders them to Fort Amsterdam. In time for a harsh winter, the tiny settlement, given the name New Amsterdam, has thirty log houses, a stone-walled company office, and a two-story horse mill for grinding bark to process pelts. The settlement is a small, distant branch of a large Dutch company.

1626   Eleven African men, probably captured from Spanish or Portuguese ships, are brought to New Amsterdam to labor as slaves for the Dutch West India Company.

The names they have been given, like d'Angola, Congo, and Portuguis Garcia, point to their origin and captors. The enslaved men can be baptized, marry, own property, and work for themselves when not required for company tasks. They can sue and bear witness against whites.

1627   A new windmill towers over the settlement and is a landmark for ships. The windmill's four sails are memorialized today on New York City's seal, along with two flour barrels, two beavers, a Lenape with bow and arrow, a sailor, and an eagle.

View of New Amsterdam shows the fort as planned, but not built. The image is reversed. New Jersey is in the background.

1627   The Dutch West India Company has trouble keeping people in the colony. The first colonists begin to abandon New Netherland.

1628   To build up its population, the company tries a new idea, offering large grants of land to wealthy patroons who can guarantee to import fifty settlers. The patrician Dutch try to institute feudalism in the New World.

1628   Three black women are brought to New Amsterdam as slaves.

1628   Preacher Jonas Michaelius, a company employee, holds Dutch Reformed Church services in the only place available, upstairs in the horse mill. In 1633 the first church will be built on Pearl Street.

1629   Desperate to succeed in the New World, the Dutch West India Company allows patroons to trade in furs for their own profit.

1630   Some settlers build an impractically large ship—600 tons—at New Amsterdam because there is more timber here than anyone can dream of.

Fur smuggling, the private trading of pelts, is common. Everyone hopes to profit from furs, and farmers quit the land to get rich quickly.

Giant American chestnut trees (*Castanea dentata*) grow to 125 feet in great stands all over the coast. It is said that a squirrel can travel from Maine to Georgia through the branches. Today the tree is almost wiped out by blight in the eastern United States.

Company-run New Amsterdam is a town of wooden structures where fire is a threat. The chimneys of many houses are only plastered wood, and the roofs are thatched with reeds.

On moonless nights every seventh building keeps a lantern lit.

A muddy inlet on Broad Street allows loaded boats to come right into town. The canal provides water for fighting fires. It stinks in summer and freezes in winter.

Beyond a rickety fence are the *bouweries*, or farms, where most of the settlement's colonists live. The Dutch are famous for both their ornamental and kitchen gardens.

1633   The new 27-year-old director-general of the company, Wouter van Twiller, arrives with a military force: 104 soldiers armed with wheel-lock muskets.

1636   Van Twiller makes the first recorded Brooklyn land deal in Midwout and Amersfoort, today Flatbush and Flatlands. The Canarsee chief Pennewits officiates for the Indians. Van Twiller's land grab will include thousands of acres—what we know today as Wards, Randalls, Roosevelt, and Governors Islands, plus huge sections of Brooklyn and a plantation in Sapokanikan, later known as the West Village, where company labor will grow superior tobacco and other crops for Van Twiller's personal profit.

1637   A patroon's great estate fails on a large island in the harbor. The island is turned over to the Dutch government (*Staaten Generaal*) to become Staten Island.

Merchant traders, forbidden by the Dutch West India Company to coin money, instead use strings of iridescent white or purple shell beads called wampum. The Lenape spiritual medium, sometimes woven into belts as a mnemonic record of agreements among peoples, or placed in graves to aid the journeys of the dead, is given a cash value.

1865 caricature of van Twiller

1638 Van Twiller, charged with alcoholism and incompetence, is succeeded by Willem Kieft. Use of alcohol, called "strong water," heralds early death for many Lenape youths.

> ❧
>
> Springs, wells, and ponds serve the freshwater needs of a small population.
>
> ❧
>
> Garbage is dumped into the narrow, muddy streets of the settlement and left for the pigs to clean up. Soon, gardens have to be fenced in to save the cabbages.

1638 The Dutch Reformed Church schoolmaster Adam Roelantsen opens a school for girls and boys, the forerunner of the Collegiate School, New York City's oldest school. Tuition: two beaver pelts a year.

1639 The patroonship system fails and is dropped. The company entirely gives up the fur monopoly. Everyone is allowed to trade, if they pay customs duties to ship out pelts. Under the new rules, colonists can have as much land as they can cultivate.

1639 The new Director-general Willem Kieft establishes the folly of his get-tough regime by taxing the Indians bushels of corn, furs, or wampum, when not even the colonists pay regular taxes. The Indians try to pay up, but nothing is good enough. From folly to war is a short step.

> ❧
>
> Settlers' cattle and hogs trample Indian maize fields. Indians hunt down livestock to protect their crops.
>
> ❧
>
> "Misunderstanding, miscalculation, and stupidity led to a wave of murders, assaults, and thefts by settlers and Indians alike. . . ." —Anthropologist Robert S. Grumet

1639 A Danish gentleman, Jonas Bronck, and his Dutch wife buy 500 acres from the Indians in what is now the Bronx, named after the Broncks.

1641 Kieft, failing in his bid to subdue all the Indians, proclaims a bounty for each Raritan Indian brought to him.

> ❧
>
> The colonists run a ferry between Manhattan and Brooklyn. Indians have traveled among the City's many islands in their watercraft for thousands of years.

1642 Fund-raising for New Amsterdam's first stone church, St. Nicholas, is begun after several rounds of drinking at a wedding. "All then with light heads subscribed largely, competing with one another."

1642 Kieft allows English settlers into the colony of New Netherland to increase its population. Their first settlement, at Maspeth in Queens, is abandoned in 1644 after attacks by the Indians.

1643 Father Isaac Jogues, a French Jesuit missionary visiting the town, writes of four or five hundred men speaking eighteen different languages on the island of Manhattan and its surroundings.

1643 The first black landowner in New Netherland is Domingo Anthony. Twenty years later he and his wife are among the first families to free slaves by buying them; they pay 300 guilders for an Angolan girl, Christina, and adopt her as their daughter.

1643 On the night of February 25, Director-general Willem Kieft's militia murders 120 Lenapes, who are on the run from other Indians and are camped on the Manhattan and Jersey shores.

1643 The Indians unite against the Dutch. The one Dutchman they trust is David de Vries, a landowner whom they call a good chief of his people. De Vries risks his life at a council of sixteen powerful Long Island chiefs at Rockaway. One of the chiefs, "the best speaker . . . began his oration in Indian," holding a bundle of sticks and counting out Dutch brutalities one by one.

1643 Seven Indian groups, numbering fifteen hundred warriors, destroy almost all of the forty farms around New Amsterdam. Two attempts at peace fail.

1643 "Among the dead were Anne Hutchinson and her children. She had fled the intolerance of New England only to meet death at the hands of the Indians incited to war by a reckless Dutch governor." —Historian Oliver Rink

1643 Anne Hutchinson has refused to heed several warnings from the Indians not to build a house on their trail. The Hutchinson River will be named for her.

> ❧
>
> Food shortages are common because of war and because farmers grow a cash crop: tobacco. Market-Field, near the fort, where corn, fish, and pelts can be bought from out-of-towners and Indians, is regulated to one day a week. Twice a year a cattle market is held.

1644 A petition against Kieft, written by the men he has chosen to advise him, is smuggled to Holland. The people are furious at Kieft's barbaric handling of the Indians, particularly since it has resulted in the devastation of their property.

1644 The eleven African men brought to New Netherland by the Dutch West India Company in 1626 petition for freedom for themselves and their wives after eighteen years of bondage. They are granted partial freedom but must still work on demand and pay a yearly fee, or tithe. The company can claim the labor of their children.

1644 The freed men and women settle near Minetta Brook (in what is now Greenwich Village), which supplies fresh water and plenty of trout.

1644 A Dutch woman, Tryntje Jonas, is paid a small salary by the Dutch West India Company for the healing of the sick.

1645 The first woman granted a town charter in the New World is Englishwoman Lady Deborah Moody, a religious refugee from Massachusetts. She and her followers establish a planned English town in the Dutch colony: Gravesend, at Coney Island. Lady Moody holds town meetings and guarantees her community freedom of worship and self government.

New Amsterdam about 1650

1645 Oratam, the great Hackensack leader, is one of the signatories of a peace treaty signed at Fort Amsterdam on August 30 to mark the end of the bitter Kieft Indian War, which has killed Europeans and at least a thousand native people. The treaty is sealed by smoking the *calumet* (ceremonial pipe) under the open sky.

1645 Kieft is sacked as director-general but cannot leave until his replacement, Peter Stuyvesant, arrives two years later.

1646 The buying and selling of human beings in New Netherland begins: the first ship of Negroes arrives from Africa via Brazil.

1646 Breuckelen is the first Dutch town to be chartered in New Netherland.

1646 Thirty-five taverns do business in tiny New Amsterdam.

1647 One-legged Peter Stuyvesant replaces Kieft as director-general. New Amsterdam and nearby settlements, diminished by war and mismanagement, are reduced to traders and a few officials and farmers. The tumble-down fort holds a garrison of a hundred men. After years of struggle, Stuyvesant's controversial eighteen-year directorship will transform New Amsterdam from a ramshackle trading post to a bustling port.

1649 "The ink freezes in the pen," writes settler Anneke Melyn in December from Staten Island. "The poor people have scarcely anything to eat, for no supplies of bread, butter, beef and pork can now be had."

> The Roosevelt family arrives in New Amsterdam. Claes Martenszen van Rosenvelt and his wife, Jannetje Samuels Thomas, settle in lower Manhattan and prosper. Their descendants include Theodore, Franklin, and Eleanor.

1649 A Remonstrance written by the New Amsterdam lawyer Adriaen van der Donck and other officials is taken to Holland to protest Stuyvesant's handling of the company. His irascible and bossy nature has riled the council, but he brings some stability to the colony.

1651 The English Navigation Act bans Dutch trade with other more powerful colonies to the north and south. The Dutch are hemmed in.

> The overextended company is bankrupt; the paradoxical Dutch can't compete with other more single-minded empires. Meanwhile, the colonists are busy trading privately for their own profit, and smuggling.

1651 Stuyvesant buys his farm, bounded by what we know as 5th and 17th Streets, the East River, and Fourth Avenue. Part of this area becomes Stuyvesant Town in the 1940s.

Dancing on the Battery

1650s Because of the settlers' growing demand for land, the Nayack chief Mattano sells his holdings in Brooklyn and leads his people to Staten Island, which the Lenapes call *Aquehonga Manacknong.*

1653 The City of New Amsterdam at last becomes a municipality in its own right, and is awarded its own seal. The City Tavern becomes City Hall, where the provincial assembly is held. The bell in the cupola marks the hours; three strokes announce the reading of a proclamation.

City Hall

Because of its silver, Potosí, Bolivia, with a population of 160,000, is the biggest city in the New World. The settlement of New Amsterdam has 800 inhabitants.

1653 The colony puts up a line of wooden palisades, 2,340 feet long, 9 feet high, and 18 inches thick, along the northern edge of town as protection against an English attack. The path beside it becomes Wall Street.

In a burst of civic improvement, Stuyvesant deepens, widens, and shores up the Heere Gracht, the canal that runs along the middle of Broad Street. Bridges span the canal, as in Amsterdam.

More and more settlers' houses are now built of brick. In the Dutch fashion, they have steep roofs and stepped gables, and at the traditional divided front door, a *stoep*, or stoop.

1654 The first Rosh Hashanah is observed here by Jews, twenty-three of whom have arrived aboard the *Sainte Catherine* from Recife, Brazil, after fleeing the Portuguese Inquisition there.

Autocratic Peter Stuyvesant does not want these newcomers. He wants to limit the practice of religion to that of the Dutch Reformed Church, but he is told he must tolerate other creeds. The company needs people, and intolerance interferes with profit.

1655 The first ship with slaves brought directly from Africa arrives.

1655 An Indian confederacy (near two thousand in strength) sweeps down the Hudson to attack the weakened Canarsee tribe. A woman with the confederacy is shot picking a peach in a Dutch orchard. In retaliation, Indians on Staten Island burn farms and many people are killed on both sides in the Peach War. More than a hundred settlers are taken prisoner by the Indians, to be released for a price over the next two years.

1655 The town of Flatbush builds the first church on Long Island.

1656 Jamaica has its European beginnings in a settlement known as Rustdorp, which, despite its name, is English.

The young women of the households do the wash on the grassy banks of a brook that empties into the East River. The path beside it is named Maiden Lane.

"The waters of the New Netherlands are rich with fishes," writes the lawyer and landowner Adriaen van der Donck in his *Description of The New Netherlands*. He lists fish from pike to sheeps-head.

Palisade on Wall Street

1657 Two Quaker women, members of the new Society of Friends, arrive in New Amsterdam and are immediately arrested and banished for praying in public. On Stuyvesant's orders another defiant Quaker is tortured, but Stuyvesant's sister-in-law, Anna Bayard, intervenes. The settlers of Flushing, led by the convert John Bowne, protest in a formal Remonstrance.

1658 The village of New Harlem is founded. Parts of Harlem itself have been farmed since 1637.

1658 Hillegond Joris is hired by the company as a midwife.

1658 The Rattle Watch patrols from 9 p.m. until morning drumbeat in orange and blue regimentals. Each of its nine members carries a musket, sword, pistol, lantern, and—to sound the alarm in case of fire or attack—a large rattle.

Stuyvesant's Great House, White Hall

❧

Bowling on the green and ice skating become favorite pastimes of a growing population.

❧

Colonists fill their memoirs with observations about the Indians. "With the fidelity and attention to detail of Dutch painters these writers describe the Indians' persons and clothing, houses, food, domestic habits and social customs." —Historian Alice Kenney

The Heere Gracht or Canal at Broad Street in 1663

1660 The first hospital is opened in two buildings on Manhattan. Lucas Santomee, whose father arrived as a slave in 1626, is a doctor there.

1660 In England, King Charles II is restored to the throne. He gives his brother, the Duke of York, all the territory between the Delaware and the Connecticut Rivers—the whole Dutch colony and more.

1661 The Quaker John Bowne builds a house in Flushing which still stands today.

Bowne allows the outlawed Quaker faith to be practiced there; in 1662 he is arrested and sent to the Netherlands. The Dutch judges acquit him of all charges. Religious freedom in America has passed its first legal test.

1663 Smallpox is often carried from one settlement to another by people running from an outbreak. An Indian messenger from the Delaware River brings the disease to New Amsterdam.

1663 The Provincial Assembly is called. Delegates from Breuckelen, Nieu Amersfoort (Flatlands), Midwout (Flatbush), Nieu Utrecht, Boswyck (Bushwick), Bergen, and New Harlem convene at New Amsterdam to unite against the English.

1664 "Between three stools one falls to the ground, as the proverb has it," writes Peter Stuyvesant, threatened by the English, the Indians, and the Swedes in Delaware, and still waiting for help from the Dutch West India Company.

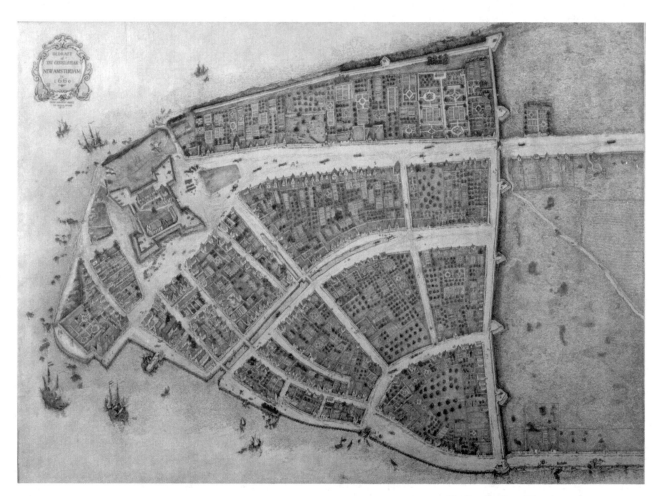

The Castello Plan of New Amsterdam

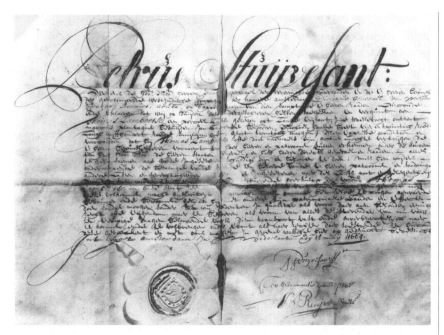

A Brooklyn land grant signed by Stuyvesant,
1664

1664 "We know no New Netherland unless you can show us a Royal Patent for it from his Majesty," writes the leader of the newly chartered Connecticut Colony to Stuyvesant.

1664 On August 26 an English force of four warships with 300 men, led by Colonel Richard Nicolls, arrives in Gravesend Bay. The sails are seen from the fort.

1664 The English offer Dutch colonists equal rights with the English and forty-eight hours to decide. In New Amsterdam gunpowder is damp, guns are broken, food supplies short, and the colonists do not wish to fight for the company.

1664 On September 8 documents are signed, and the City changes hands without a shot fired. Fort Amsterdam becomes Fort James. New Amsterdam becomes New York. Richard Nicolls is governor.

❧

Dutch foods still popular in today's New York are *koolsla* (cole slaw), *olykoecks* (doughnuts), cookies, crullers, and waffles.

❧

Dutch names still in everyday use are Harlem, Brooklyn, Van Cortlandt, Dyckman Street, Bowery, Spuyten Duyvil, Bruckner Boulevard, Amsterdam Avenue, Staten Island, and the Kill van Kull.

The English settle in . . .

1664 In October every Dutch colonist swears allegiance as a subject of the King of England. Not one settler returns to Europe, and only the Dutch troops must leave. Peter Stuyvesant lives out his life in New York City.

1664 New York's fifteen hundred people are Dutch, English, Flemish, Walloon, French Huguenot, German, Danish, Swedish, African, Jewish. New England is known for its homogeneity, New York for its pluralism.

1665 The Duke's Laws give the colony a small taste of self-rule. Thirty-four delegates from seventeen towns approve the new English code.

Pearl and Chatham Streets about 1670

The Lenapes are being driven out. Leaders buy time for their people using the only power they have left, the threat of war, and land the Europeans badly want. Ten square miles can be exchanged for blankets and awls.

1666 Sara Kierstede, a European interpreter, speaks trade jargon and Munsee and translates for the great Hackensack leader Oratam.

1668 ". . . this Citty of New yorke . . . lyes now groaning under the afflicting hand of Gods last Judgment." Governor Lovelace declares a day of atonement for the swearing and impiety he thinks are responsible for the latest epidemic, probably malaria or typhoid.

Settlers reaffirm yearly the boundaries of their deeds in response to the Indian way of landholding. To be on the safe side, Europeans repurchase the same land over and over again—for example, Fordham in the Bronx.

New York remains very Dutch. The old Dutch families hold sway, and it is twenty-five years before New York becomes a really English town.

1670 Governor Lovelace makes the final purchase of Staten Island from the Indians for 2,400 feet of strung wampum, 30 shirts, 30 kettles, 20 guns, a small barrel of powder, 60 bars of lead, 30 axes, 30 hoes, and 50 knives. Indian children as well as adults sign the deed to perpetuate the memory of the land deal.

1670s Money is still in short supply because the colonies are not allowed to coin their own, so while fines are levied in guilders, they are paid in beaver pelts or wampum.

1670 The City is given control of the Hudson River carrying trade by Lovelace.

1672 Peter Stuyvesant dies and is buried under his chapel, now the site of St. Marks Church in the Bowery.

1673 The first postal service in America begins. Once a month a rider carries letters by land between New York and Boston.

1673 Eight Dutch warships anchor off Staten Island in August. The ships' guns fire on Fort James; helped by Dutch residents, the Dutch snatch back New York City for the next fifteen months and name it New Orange.

1674 New Orange becomes New York again by treaty. The Dutch political chapter of the City's history is over.

1676 The Great Dock on the East River is built. Its two arms provide a small, safe harbor from Water Street to Coenties Slip. The dock is used until 1750.

The Great Dock

1679 Almost 70 percent of Indian land is owned by Europeans. Rechgawawank Indians, who once camped in upper Manhattan, ask for continued use of their planting grounds. Their ceremonial rock shelters and shell heaps can be seen today on walking tours of Inwood Park.

1680 A magnificent comet frightens and awes everyone.

1680 New York capitalizes on its excellent Dutch flour. The Bolting Act requires all flour shipped from New York to be pro-cessed and packed in the City. This monopoly triples the City's wealth and population within twenty years, hence the flour barrels on the City seal.

1680s "Take new cream two gallons, beat it up to a thicknesse, then add half a pint of orange-flower-water, and as much red wine." Orange butter is a favorite treat of the day and also a pomade.

1682 Jews, allowed a new burial ground outside City walls, open Chatham Square Cemetery, which still stands today, its tombstones bearing their Spanish, Portuguese, and Hebrew inscriptions.

> Oysters, mussels, clams, and scallops provide a rich natural harvest of the waterways for Europeans and Indians alike.

1683 The Duke of York names a Catholic governor, Thomas Dongan, and allows him to call an assembly of seventeen elected representatives from ten New York counties.

Brooklyn Ferry landing

Tombstone in Chatham Square Cemetery, 1683

Debajo desta lossa sepultado	[Beneath this stone lies buried
Yasse, Binjamin Bueno de Mesq^{ta}	Benjamin Bueno de Mesquita
Falesio y deste mundo fue tomado	He died and his blessed soul was taken
En qatro de hesvan su almo benditta	From this world on the fourth of Heshvan
Aquy de los vivientes apartado	Here from the living separated
Espera por tu dios que resusita	Wait for thy God who revives
Los muertos de su pueblo con piadades	The dead of his people in mercy
Para biuir sin fin de eternidades	To live eternally without end]

5444

1683 The Assembly adopts the Charter of Libertyes and Priviledges, a modern Magna Carta. The Duke hopes that self-representation will make the colony profitable. He gives the nod to self-taxation, freedom of conscience, and trial by jury, but within three years he reneges on these rights.

1683 Kings County—today's borough of Brooklyn—is named after King Charles II. Queens County is named for his queen, Catherine of Braganza, and Richmond County—Staten Island—for his illegitimate son, the Duke of Richmond.

1684 Governor Dongan approves a new municipal government that divides New York City (Manhattan) into six wards, each to elect an alderman. For 200 years wards are the basic unit of City politics.

1685 Charles II dies and the disliked Duke of York becomes King James II. New York changes from a ducal proprietary to a royal province. Within three years the king makes New York a part of New England and, to the fury of New Yorkers, all the City's public records are packed off to Boston.

1688 The Glorious Revolution in England replaces Catholic King James with Protestant William III of Orange from the Netherlands. News travels slowly. King James's man is still governor of New York.

1689 Rumors abound in a society where hearsay is the chief source of news. New Yorkers are afraid that the City will be handed over to Catholic France and burned to the ground. In their panic they turn to their own military leadership for protection.

1689 New York City's militia seizes Fort James from the English garrison. The militia captain Jacob Leisler is chosen to be commander in chief of the province. Farmers and laborers support Leisler's Rebellion against the Catholics, the English, and the wealthy.

1691 Leisler becomes tyrannical. Rich merchants turn on Leisler and his son-in-law Jacob Milborne and have them hanged by the authorities.

1691 Bronx frontiersmen are "rude and heathenish" to an observer who is shocked that they spend Sundays hunting, fishing, and drinking at the tavern.

1692 The tradition of religious tolerance in New York pays off, while Salem in Massachusetts endures witch trials.

1693 New York City's first printing press is set up by the royal printer William Bradford, who has just come from Philadelphia.

1693 King's Bridge joins Manhattan to the mainland, the Bronx.

The Dutch feast day of Sint Nikolaas, December 6, is a children's holiday with gifts. English New York changes "Sint Nikolaas" to Santa Claus and appropriates the saint for Christmas.

Boats in the East River

The Burgis View of New York City, 1717

1690s Governor Benjamin Fletcher encourages smuggling, skims funds for his own profit, and allows pirates to remain in port. The colony prospers.

1694 The Quaker Meeting House is built in Flushing, Queens, and is still in use three centuries later.

1696 Captain Kidd, married and living in a grand house on Pearl Street, with a country house on East 74th Street and a pew in Trinity Church, sails off for the Crown to capture pirates. He reverts to piracy and is hanged in London five years later. His treasure has yet to be found.

1698 Anglicanism is made the official religion of the colony. Trinity Church, founded by royal charter from William III, holds its first services at Broadway and Wall Street. It is a club for the small but powerful English community.

1702 Stuyvesant's nephew Nicholas Bayard, who pushed for Jacob Leisler's execution, is freed of treason charges. The bitter divisions of the rebellion begin to fade and the wealthy English now have a firm hold on power.

1702 Yellow fever kills 570 New Yorkers.

A Dutch farmhouse

Until the American Revolution, the people of Brooklyn mostly speak Dutch. Brooklyn is still rural with small farms worked by indentured servants and African slaves. The farmhouse is "a one-story gabled affair built of wood or stone, lighted by narrow windows and protected by strong palisades against wild beasts and Indian prowlers . . . the floors [are] carpeted with white sand, brought from nearby beaches." —Writers Grace Glueck and Paul Gardner

&

City gentlemen don powdered wigs and dress in scarlet, blue, and green hose and silk breeches; their jackets are embroidered with gold and silver thread. They make quite a contrast to drab New Englanders.

&

Dutch women dress plainly but love jewelry. According to a Boston visitor, they wear earrings with "Jewells of a large size and many in number. And their fingers hoop't with Rings."

1703 A new City Hall is built on Wall Street, facing south down Broad Street. It will be renamed Federal Hall in time for George Washington's inauguration in 1789.

1708 Governor Lord Cornbury distresses New Yorkers by stealing from City coffers and regularly appearing in his wife's dresses. He is finally removed from office for failing to make the colony profitable to the Crown.

1712 Trinity Church, society's bastion, no longer permits African burials in its churchyard, so Africans bury their dead near the Fresh Water Pond, also known as the Collect, almost a mile north of Wall Street. Laws limit funeral gatherings to twelve people. (See 1991)

1712 During an uprising by African slaves, eight whites are killed. Nineteen blacks are executed by barbaric medieval methods. A new law prohibits Africans from owning property.

&

Slavery under the Dutch was a jumble of practices. The Dutch often worked alongside their slaves. The English have institutionalized slavery with a vengeance. Violence against rebelling blacks is brutal.

&

The remaining native people are forced to leave their homesites and choicest fishing camps and move into the uplands to face old enemies. In 1701 one Wiechquaesgeck woman, Karacapacomont, signs away final rights to her homeland in the Bronx.

&

". . . it is to be admired how strangely they [the Indians] have decreast by the Hand of God, since the English first settling." —Chronicler Daniel Denton

The slave market (left) and the old City Hall

1714 Governor Robert Hunter improves many aspects of the City, from finances to ferries, by taxing residents. He writes a farce, *Androboros*, which is the first play to be printed in English in the colonies.

England's choice of governors after Hunter is a farce; men without common sense or experience are appointed. The City thrives anyway. The island of Manhattan will have 7,000 people in 1720, 11,000 in 1741.

1725 The royal printer William Bradford starts New York's first newspaper, the *New York Gazette*.

1728 George II's Scottish friend John Montgomerie, governor for three years, builds up City revenues with a barrage of new fees. Merchants bribe him to get what they want. A new City charter extends the council's powers as well as the City limits.

1730 The Jewish congregation, Shearith Israel, established here in 1654, at last has a synagogue, on Mill Street.

1731 Smallpox kills 500, including Governor Montgomerie, and the council runs the City government.

1731 Two fire engines (hand pumpers) arrive from London. They are vital to a city where few can afford to build in brick or stone.

Snuff, made from flavored ground tobacco, becomes a profitable commodity.

Painters and limners, like those in the old Dutch Duyckinck family, paint portraits of the wealthy and their children.

As American as apple pie: the Newtown Pippin, grown in Queens, is the first apple exported to England, where it sells for a high price.

New York becomes a center for sugar refining. Families like the Bayards, Livingstons, Roosevelts, Stewarts, and Van Cortlandts make good money from sugar.

In the 1730s nearly fifteen hundred slaves are brought to the City, and the slave markets at the foot of Wall Street are named after prominent Dutch and English families in the rapidly growing slave trade.

1731 An early attempt at a public library is at City Hall on Wall Street, with 1,642 books owned by the Society for the Propagation of the Gospel in Foreign Parts.

1732 Colonel William Cosby, Montgomerie's successor, begins to raise hackles.

1733 The City creates a bowling green and rents it to citizens for one peppercorn a year. Present-day Bowling Green, the oldest park in the City, is enclosed with an iron fence dating from 1771.

1733 Printer William Bradford's former apprentice, a German named John Peter Zenger, starts the feisty, satirical *New-York Weekly Journal* with the support of wealthy merchants who are furious over Governor Cosby's thoughtless tyranny.

1734 Cosby jails Zenger for slander and burns copies of the *Journal*. Zenger's wife, Anna Catherine, runs the paper while he is in jail.

The Collect Pond, 1798

The Commons, used since the mid-1600s for grazing, begins to change. New York builds its first poorhouse on the land that today is City Hall Park.

1735   Governor Cosby disbars New York attorneys who plan to defend Zenger, so Zenger's supporters bring in the gifted defense lawyer Andrew Hamilton from Philadelphia. In the first libel trial in the colonies, Zenger is acquitted because the facts he printed about Cosby are true. Freedom of the press is established. Hamilton tells the jury, "It is not the cause of a poor printer, nor of New York alone which you are now trying. . . . No! It is the best cause; it is the cause of liberty, both of exposing and opposing arbitrary power by speaking and writing the truth!"

1737   An earthquake rattles New York.

1741   New York endures its own version of witch trials. In the aftermath of a second slave rebellion, thirteen slaves are burned at the stake, eighteen hanged, and seventy-one deported for allegedly conspiring to burn down the colony. Two white men and two white women are also hanged. The gallows is on a little island in the Collect Pond. The stake is between two hills a short distance away.

Slaves sell for forty to fifty pounds and have an import duty of forty shillings. Elderly slaves are often freed to save on upkeep, and some become beggars.

One out of five of the City's residents is African.

1741   The City water supply is stretched beyond the limit. New wells are dug, and the City supplies the pumps. The Tea Water Pump fills kettles on Chatham Street, and its clean water is carted about the City for sale.

Tea Water Pump

1742 A neighborhood patrol gives rich and poor men alike the burden of night duty, but the rich can pay for substitutes. Crimes to watch for: gambling, prostitution, and drunkenness, as well as robbery, assault, and murder.

1742 Forty-four volunteer firefighters stand at the ready. The volunteer system lasts until the 1860s.

1747 About a hundred mechanics protest that workers from neighboring colonies are undercutting the wage scale.

1750 An English company puts on Shakespeare's *Richard III* at the New Theater on Nassau Street.

1750 Thousands of hogs snort and root through City streets.

Fraunces Tavern, 1779

1754 Wealthy English New Yorkers give their City prestige by founding two major institutions, King's College (renamed Columbia after the Revolution) and the New York Society Library. The college, whose first class of eight meets at Trinity Church, builds its endowment from public lotteries. The New York Society Library is operating today in an Italian palazzo-style building on East 79th Street.

1756 In a major victory for New York, the British Parliament allows New York's assembly to control the colony's budget.

1758 To halt epidemics, incoming ships are quarantined until inspected, and a pesthouse on Bedloe's Island confines people with highly contagious diseases.

1760 The colonies' first recognized black poet is New York's Jupiter Hammon.

1760 An examination and a license are now required to practice medicine.

1761 Only about 10 percent of the City's population has the right to vote. Freeholders may vote, but only if they pay. As in all the colonies, women and blacks are not eligible. Elections in each of the wards are by a show of hands.

1762 Oil lampposts light City streets with their fitful glow. Gas street lighting is still sixty years off.

1762 Samuel Fraunces, a Caribbean immigrant, purchases a building for use as a tavern. Today Fraunces Tavern at Pearl and Broad Streets, famous for its part in the American Revolution and the early republic, is rebuilt as a museum.

1763 Delawares (or Lenapes), exiled from their East Coast homeland at the end of the seven-year French and Indian War, are forced to move west. They settle in Wisconsin, Oklahoma, and Ontario. Those few who hold on in the City live quietly in back lots in Washington Heights, Staten Island, and Canarsie; they intermarry and their customs die out in a generation.

1763 With a population of about 18,000, New York is a prosperous colonial port with wharves along the East and Hudson Rivers. Despite England's rules it trades wherever profit is to be had. It is second only to Philadelphia in importance.

Here comes the Revolution . . .

1763 The Treaty of Paris, concluding the French and Indian War in the northeastern United States, confirms English control of North America. But the war has been expensive, and the colonies refuse to pay for it. England decides to end its "salutary neglect" and takes a new hard line.

1764 Britain passes the restrictive Sugar Act and prohibits the colonies from issuing paper money.

1765 Two public gardens, Vauxhall and its rival Ranelagh, open just outside the growing town. Attractions include band concerts, fireworks, and afternoon tea.

1765 In response to the Stamp Act, which taxes everyday life by requiring stamps on forty-two different kinds of documents, a new organization, the Sons of Liberty, riots and burns the lieutenant governor in effigy.

A southwest view of the City about 1763

1765 With nine colonies represented, the Stamp Act Congress convenes at City Hall on Wall Street, denounces the Stamp Act, and adopts a declaration of rights and grievances of the colonists in America.

1766 The first New York blood of the Revolution is shed. The patriots—the Sons of Liberty—raise one of their liberty poles (tall pine poles bearing messages of freedom) on the Commons. British soldiers tear down the pole and wound several patriots.

1766 St. Paul's Chapel is completed six blocks up Broadway from Trinity Church. It still stands today, the oldest church building in Manhattan.

St. Paul's Chapel in its 1837 setting

27

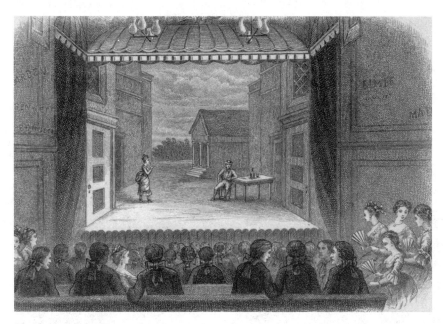

The Theatre in John Street

1767   The Theatre in John Street opens and will become the best-known playhouse in the City.

1768   In a meeting at Fraunces Tavern, twenty merchants create the New York Chamber of Commerce.

1770   Although most of the colonies have agreed not to trade with England, only the City takes the boycott seriously.

1771   New York Hospital receives a charter from King George III. It is in operation today on the Upper East Side as the City's oldest medical institution.

1772   In thirty years the City's population has doubled to 22,000. There's a tavern for every fifty-five people.

1773   England has been tightening its grip with the Quartering Act, New York Restraining Act, and the Townshend Revenue Acts. Now, in the midst of an economic slump, the Tea Act. Furious New Yorkers hold a mass meeting at City Hall.

1774   New Yorkers have a tea party, storming a ship in the harbor and dumping eighteen boxes of tea, although those busy costuming themselves as Mohawks in imitation of the Bostonian protest miss taking part.

1774   An engineer is hired by the City to solve the acute water shortage. Because of the Revolution, his plan will not be implemented until 1799.

1774   At the pro-English Committee of Fifty-One, a college student named Alexander Hamilton rebelliously calls for a congress of the thirteen colonies to deal with Britain's aggressive actions.

1775   New York's new Provincial Congress votes to enlist patriot troops and fortify the City against a British attack.

1776   Having forced the British out of Boston, George Washington's army arrives in New York.

> "The City was becoming increasingly radical and attempted to speak for the entire province, much as Paris did for France in its revolutions." —Historians George J. Lankevich and Howard B. Furer

1776 As they celebrate the Declaration of Independence, New York patriots topple the statue of George III on Bowling Green. Its two tons of lead are carted up to Connecticut to be recycled into musketballs.

1776 General George Washington urges patriots to evacuate the city.

1776 An immense British fleet anchors in the harbor with 45,000 soldiers and seamen (British and Hessian). Twenty-one thousand of these men land in Brooklyn and take thirteen hundred American prisoners in the Battle of Brooklyn.

1776 Washington's remaining nine thousand troops in Brooklyn escape across the East River in the dark of night. Lieutenant Aaron Burr leads them to northern Manhattan, where, in the Battle of Harlem Heights, they stop the British temporarily.

1776 Benjamin Franklin and John Adams try to negotiate a settlement with the British. The meeting, which is a failure, is held at a solid stone house (circa 1680) on the southern tip of Staten Island. This house is now a museum in Conference House Park.

Patriot Nathan Hale, a Yale graduate, records in Latin the placement of the British troops in Harlem. The British hang him as a spy near Chambers Street. "I only regret that I have but one life to lose for my country," he says.

The first American woman to fight in the Revolution is Margaret Corbin, who takes over her wounded husband's cannon post at what is now Fort Tryon Park on upper Broadway.

Patriots toppling the Statue of King George III

1776 Washington's forces try one last time to wrench New York from the British and are defeated. At Fort Washington 2,800 troops are taken prisoner. New York is in British hands for the next seven years. It is their command center and prisoner of war compound. It is also a Tory refuge and a haven for runaway slaves.

1776 Three thousand prostitutes are shipped from Liverpool for the 25,000 British and Hessian troops occupying New York.

The British use a fleet of ships moored on the Brooklyn side of the East River in Wallabout Bay to house the patriot prisoners. These ships "caused more deaths than all the land and sea battles and campaigns in all the years of the American Revolution combined.... It is believed that eleven thousand American prisoners died aboard the rotting ships in New York Harbor, far more than the 6,824 American troops killed in combat." —Historian Kenneth T. Jackson

1776, 1778 Two fires, possibly the result of arson on the part of patriots trying to destroy the British stronghold, burn down a third of the City.

1780 The harbor freezes over during an unusually severe winter.

1781 The Revolution is won with the help of the French at Yorktown, Virginia.

1783 During an exodus that takes eight months, nearly 35,000 Loyalists and free blacks leave through the port of New York.

The British attack on Fort Washington

1783 The Treaty of Paris recognizes the United States as a nation. On November 25, for many years celebrated as Evacuation Day, the British redcoats officially leave New York, and General Washington and Governor George Clinton march the bedraggled patriot troops triumphantly from northern Manhattan to the Battery.

Washington Entering New York, 1783

An American city . . .

1783 The City is a burned-out shell, a shadow of its former self. In the years following the Revolution, it makes a strong recovery in commerce and population and is virtually rebuilt. Confiscation of Loyalist land pays the bills.

1783 The British forces have left, and the Irish Catholics start coming.

1784 A twenty-year-old German immigrant, John Jacob Astor, comes to the City and gets a job as a baker's boy. A young woman he meets while she's scrubbing her mother's front steps will help him advance with her dowry, good business sense, and Brevoort family connections.

1785 New York City is made the first capital of the United States. City Hall on Wall Street is renovated and renamed Federal Hall.

1785 The New York Manumission Society is founded by a roster of prominent men to prod the public into abolishing slavery, an institution that doesn't square with the ideals of the Revolution.

1785 William Dyckman builds the farmhouse still standing on 204th Street and Broadway.

1786 More than a hundred years after the first Catholic Mass was celebrated in New York, Roman Catholics are finally allowed to build a church, St. Peter's, on Barclay at Church Street.

1787 Erasmus Hall, a private school for Dutch farmers' children, opens in Brooklyn. A century later it becomes a public high school.

The Dyckman House

1787 Alexander Hamilton begins speaking out for New York's ratification of the United States Constitution. In their *Federalist* essays, Hamilton, James Madison, and John Jay express a fervent belief in the idea of a strong central government with checks and balances.

1788 New York State ratifies the Constitution.

1788 The Society of St. Tammany is founded by an upholsterer and other craftsmen as a counterpoint to an exclusive Revolutionary officers' club. Tammany gives the common soldier his own club, named after the legendary Delaware chief Tamamend. Rank in the club, using Indian titles, ranges from braves to sachems. In the early 1800s Tammany Hall backs progressive ideas such as the vote for all men (not just property holders) and the end of debtors' prison.

Alexander Hamilton during the Revolution

1788 During the two-day Doctors' Riot, three people are killed when 5,000 demonstrators mob laboratories to express outrage at purported grave-robbing for dissection.

1788 The City cracks down on taverns for cock fighting, gambling, billiards, and dice.

1789 Guns and bells herald America's new era. The first Congress under the Constitution is held in Federal Hall on Wall Street. George Washington, the first president of the United States of America, is inaugurated on the balcony. James Madison stands up in Federal Hall to propose ten amendments to the Constitution, giving the country its Bill of Rights.

1789 Imagine a city of "tattered beggars, silk-stockinged rich men, pompadoured ladies and their liveried footmen, leather-aproned mechanics and shabby apprentice-boys, sleek coach horses, pigs. It was a volatile, contentious, politicized place, where the riotous world of the laboring poor surrounded a small, self-enclosed enclave of the wealthy and urbane." —Historian Christine Stansell

1790 Secretary of the Treasury Alexander Hamilton, fearing that the deficit incurred by the Revolution will tear apart the new country, makes a deal with Thomas Jefferson, a Virginian. New York will give up its role as the nation's capital if the South will help pay off the debt. President Washington leaves his City residence for Philadelphia, the next temporary seat of government.

1790 "When all is done, it will not be Broadway," remarks Abigail Adams. The vice president's wife reconciles herself to Philadelphia.

Washington's Inauguration at Federal Hall

George Washington by Gilbert Stuart (1796)

1791 *Charlotte Temple, A Tale of Truth* by Susanna Rowson is the story of an English schoolgirl brought to New York City, where her seducer abandons her and she dies in childbirth. The popular novel captures women's fear of being a victim in a city that is rushing ahead into the future.

1790s The two greatest dangers to the City are fire and disease, both due to the critically inadequate water supply.

1792 Twenty-two stockbrokers and merchants sign the Buttonwood Agreement, establishing the forerunner of the New York Stock Exchange. The merchants meet under the buttonwood tree on Wall Street. This tree is also called sycamore or plane tree (*Platanus occidentalis*).

The Buttonwood Agreement

1792 Banished Tories are allowed to return, although they cannot claim their confiscated property. Lands once owned by Tories like the de Lancey family are divided up into lots the size of city blocks. They give us street names like Delancey Street.

1794 Bellevue Hospital for contagious diseases is opened on an estate with a beautiful East River view.

1796 Black congregants split off from the white John Street Church. In 1821 this group will form the African Methodist Episcopal Zion Church, eventually a major independent black organization.

1796 The Tontine Coffee House opens as the headquarters of a stock-based insurance company. The profit-sharing plan, or tontine, assesses and insures property such as enslaved human beings and ships.

Burr's Manhattan Company reservoir

The Tontine Coffee House

1797 New York's state capital, here for fourteen years, leaves town for Albany.

1797 The dollar, the dime, and the cent are introduced, though the use of shillings and pence continues well into the next century.

1797 The death penalty for "lusts of men with men and women with women," on the books since 1665, is abolished.

1797 Washington Square is the City's new potter's field. As the City expands northward, Madison Square and Bryant Park provide space for thousands more burials. Hart Island in Long Island Sound has been the burial ground for the City's poor since 1869.

1797 Yellow fever in Philadelphia drives President John Adams to take refuge with his daughter in the Bronx for the summer. He runs the government from her farmhouse until the epidemic wanes.

1798 Yellow fever is now a regular feature of city summers. This year 2,086 New Yorkers die. A tropical mosquito (*Aedes aegypti*), brought in ships' bilge water, is responsible, but people blame bad air, filth, and the habits of the poor.

1799 New York State's Act for the Gradual Emancipation of Negroes and Other Slaves is passed.

1799 The new Manhattan Company provides some water for the City. By 1800 a reservoir with a steam pump supplies 400 houses via six miles of wooden pipes.

1799 Aaron Burr is a founder of the Manhattan Company. A loophole in the charter enables him to open a bank by the same name. Burr wants a bank so that he can sell property to the propertyless and cull their votes for his presidential campaign. In 1955 the Manhattan Company will merge with Chase National and become Chase Manhattan.

A street vendor about 1840

1801 The Brooklyn Navy Yard is opened at Wallabout Bay by the federal government. It outfits ships to capture pirates and later, during the War of 1812, to raid British merchant ships.

1803 New York City's exports increase by more than 500 percent over the next four years.

1804 The New-York Historical Society is formed by Mayor De Witt Clinton and others to preserve American and New York State historical materials. Its first home is in Federal Hall on Wall Street. It is the City's oldest continuously operating museum and is now housed on Central Park West at 77th Street.

1804 Aaron Burr is thwarted by his rival, Alexander Hamilton, one time too many and kills him in a duel. Hamilton deliberately misses his opponent.

Irish political exiles and enterprising merchants establish a social and commercial toehold vital to later mass Irish immigration. By 1860 about a third of the City will be Irish.

1805 Lorenzo da Ponte, librettist for Mozart's *The Marriage of Figaro*, *Don Giovanni*, and *Così Fan Tutte*, moves to New York to promote Italian culture. He inspires the building of the magnificent Italian Opera House (1833) and can be credited with making New York City a center for opera.

1805 The City's ice harvesting industry begins. Huge blocks of ice are packed in sawdust and shipped to Martinique in the Caribbean. By the 1880s nearly two million tons of ice a year are sold in the City itself.

1806 The Free School Society (later called the Public School Society) begins educating the children of the poor. By mid-century it has merged with other schools and enrolls 25,000 children a year.

1806 On Christmas night a nativist mob threatens the Irish Catholic congregants of St. Peter's Church. Hatred of immigrants fuels the first of many attacks on the Irish in the City.

Street cries of vendors hawking strawberries, milk, cakes, and hot corn compete with the noise of construction, traffic, ringing bells, horses, pigs, and dogs.

35

Fulton's steamboat Clermont

1807 The world's first successful steam-powered vessel, Robert Fulton's *Clermont*, makes a demonstration run on the Hudson River. It was built in a Manhattan shipyard.

1807 *The Picture of New-York* by Dr. Samuel L. Mitchill lists the four hospitals, five banks, six markets, nineteen newspapers, one theater, and the various public gardens in the City in the first guide book to New York.

1808 Rumors of war prompt feverish fort-building, and twenty-seven new fortifications sprout up over the next six years. Castle Williams on Governors Island, built to defend the City from the British in the War of 1812, still stands today.

1809 With the repeal of an old law, blacks may now pass down property to their children.

1809 *A History of New York*, a spoof by "Diedrich Knickerbocker," gives the author Washington Irving his first best-seller and the City, literary cachet. The name Knickerbocker catches on as a name for New Yorkers. Gotham is the author's satirical name for New York City as a place of wise or not-so-wise fools.

1811 The Commissioners' Plan divides almost all of Manhattan Island into blocks, using a grid system. Unlike some grand European cities, New York is planned for real estate sales, and the result is a more democratic and less intimidating cityscape.

1811 Manhattan begins to shave down many of its hills to serve the grid idea, but Broadway stays diagonal and Greenwich Village insists on keeping its crooked colonial streets.

1811 The Collect, the freshwater pond now badly polluted, is filled in, a project that provides jobs for increasing numbers of out-of-work poor.

> ❧
>
> This fill soon begins to sink, and the Five Points neighborhood, packed with immigrants, grows up near there. Today both pond and slum are gone, and Foley Square with its courthouses marks the site of the Collect.

1812 A new City Hall, "a splendid little palace," is built in a triangular park a ten-minute walk north of Wall Street. It is built of marble (except for the back) and faces south over the City. It is topped with a cupola, dome, and statue of Justice. City government is still directed from this building more than 186 years later.

1813 The British blockade the port of New York in the War of 1812. Foreign trade comes to a halt until peace is declared in 1815.

1814 Columbia University gets a present from New York State: a piece of rural Manhattan from 48th to 51st Streets, Fifth to Sixth Avenues, and holds onto it even though it seems worthless. Rockefeller Center is later built on this land.

1815 Free vaccination against smallpox is begun by the City.

1816 Brooklyn is incorporated as a village. The City of Brooklyn will be chartered in 1834.

The "splendid little palace," City Hall

1816 An English visitor remarks on the City's "wooden houses, the smallness, but neatness of the churches, the colored people, the custom of smoking segars in the streets (even followed by some of the children) and the number and nuisance of the pigs permitted to be at large."

1817 James and John Harper, Brooklyn brothers, start a printing firm; soon the firm is the largest book publisher in the United States, using high-speed roller presses to print its illustrated books.

1818 A Swedish visitor notes the dead cats and dogs in the streets "which make the air very bad."

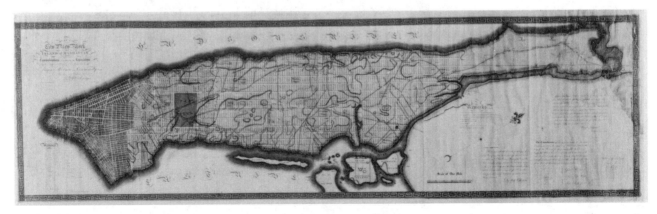

The Commissioners' 1811 plan

1818   Brooks Brothers' forerunner opens at Cherry and Catherine Streets. The company later profits as a supplier of Union military uniforms during the Civil War.

1819   The two-wheel velocipede is banned on sidewalks and in other public places.

1819   A Frenchman, Monsieur Guille, ascends to 9,000 feet in a balloon from the Vauxhall Gardens. He lands across the East River by parachute.

1820   Fire hoses have officially replaced the outdated bucket brigade.

Old leather fire buckets

1820   New York City, which consists only of Manhattan, is now the nation's largest city, with a population of 123,706.

1820   The Mercantile Library opens to give thousands of young men laboring as clerks an acceptable place to spend their evenings. It thrives, and its doors are still open today on East 47th Street.

New York merchants corner the cotton trade. Their ships take cotton from the South to the dark satanic mills of England; they pick up textiles and other goods and head home. New York makes big money on customs duties.

Eli Whitney's cotton gin (invented in 1792) and huge supplies of capital from New York merchants turn cotton into a boom crop, but make southern planters dependent upon New York finesse.

1821   The new state constitution allows white men without property to vote. This shifts power, especially in New York City, and the political machine gets going.

The Mercantile Library

1822   The first treadmill in the country is custom-built for a City prison, and twelve inmates, jailed for being poor, grind forty-five bushels of corn a day on it. (See 1831)

1822   Yellow fever drives people out of the City as far as Greenwich Village. By 1825 this outpost has grown to merge with the City.

1823   The New York Gas Light Company demonstrates gas lighting for households. In 1825 street lights begin to use gas instead of oil.

1825   The Park Theatre presents America's first grand opera, a performance of Rossini's *The Barber of Seville*.

Erie Canal celebration

1825 The Big Ditch, as the new Erie Canal is called, revolutionizes New York commerce and opens the port of New York to the Great Lakes via the Hudson River. The City celebrates. Governor De Witt Clinton steams from Buffalo to New York City, where he pours a barrel of Lake Erie water into the Atlantic Ocean.

> "The canal brought to New York City the monopoly of a rich trade, which enabled that port to wrest from Philadelphia all hope of ever again becoming the metropolis of the New World." —Historian I. N. Phelps Stokes

1827 Horse-drawn buses, called "accommodations," with room for twelve passengers, provide the first public transportation for City dwellers.

1827 The philanthropist and civic leader Joanna Bethune opens a church-based daycare center for 180 children, one to five years old.

1827 The first African American newspaper in the United States, *Freedom's Journal*, is established in New York to fight for the end of slavery and for American citizenship for blacks.

1827 New York State abolishes slavery. It is the next to the last northern state to do so.

1827 Freed black people make their homes in a Brooklyn area that becomes Weeksville, one of the first major settlements of free blacks in the north. It thrives until the 1880s. The Hunterfly Road Historic Houses seen there today are from this era.

1827 From swampy land to execution ground to potter's field, Washington Square becomes a City public park and military parade ground. The heavy artillery sometimes breaks through to the graves beneath.

1829 Fanny Wright, labeled the Great Red Harlot of Infidelity, demands legal rights for married women, accessible birth control, and educational opportunities for women. Her demands appear in the *Free Enquirer*, which she publishes with the Scottish reformer Robert Dale Owen.

1830 The United States Congress makes abortion a crime. The following year, an Englishwoman, Ann Trow Lohman (later Madame Restell), moves to New York City. She will eventually provide abortion services to women of all social classes. (See 1864)

1830 The City's population of 202,589—that's still just Manhattan—will quadruple in the next thirty years, swelled by the uprooted and impoverished of northern and western Europe—Germany and Ireland.

1830 For the next thirty years, clothing is the City's fastest-growing industry. Immigrants sew for subsistence. German immigrants start taking piecework home.

1830 A City ordinance forbids burials below Canal Street.

1830 The first American-made steam locomotive for service on the railroads is built at the West Point Foundry in Manhattan for Charleston, South Carolina.

1830s Cast-iron water mains begin to replace wooden pipes.

The Seventh Regiment drilling in Washington Square about 1851

1830s "From the 1830s on, many of the lofts put up for warehousing and the textile trades were miracles of refinement, lightness, economy, and grace. There was nothing like them elsewhere in America . . . the cast iron fronts, the wide open glass walls. . . . the best and purest that New York can offer are the commercial buildings which were formed as a perfect response to contemporary needs, in that hour of inspired invention." —Historian Nathan Silver

1831 New York University is founded as an alternative to upper-crust Episcopal Columbia.

1831 Imprisonment for insolvency is forbidden in New York State. The reformer Joseph Fay crusades for the idea that debt is not the result of moral failure.

1831 Union Square Park opens, its surrounding streets soon to be lined with mansions and theaters.

1832 Close to 4,000 New Yorkers die in the first of the City's cholera epidemics. The dreaded disease returns to kill thousands in 1834, 1849, 1854, and 1866.

1832 The New York & Harlem Rail Road runs horsecars on the Bowery from Prince to 14th Streets. The cars, which seat thirty passengers, are the first in the nation to run on iron rails. By 1837 rails are laid all the way to Harlem, a country village. Riders can go from downtown to Harlem for twenty-five cents, but must switch from horses to steam engines at the 27th Street depot.

1833 City newspapers sell for six cents, but *The Sun* costs only a penny.

1833 The new American Anti-Slavery Society, founded by blacks and whites, is based in the City. Its black speakers alert northern and western audiences to the idea that free blacks cannot become real citizens until the country abolishes slavery.

1833 Craft unions join forces in the new General Trades Union of the City of New York. The union helps establish the country's first national labor organization, which will not survive the Panic of 1837.

1834 White day workers—journeymen—vent their fury at white abolitionists and blacks in a week of violent rioting.

1834 The Brevoorts, a wealthy New York family, build a mansion on Fifth Avenue just north of Washington Square Park. Fifth Avenue will surpass Broadway as the fashionable address.

1835 In just two years, the value of property in Greenwich Village has increased more than fourfold.

1835 The Great Fire destroys the City's commercial center south of Wall Street. A fierce gale spreads the flames, and water supplies are frozen. Among the 674 buildings lost are the Merchants Exchange, the South Dutch Church, and almost all that remained of the old Dutch city. Twenty-three of the City's twenty-six fire insurance companies go bankrupt paying out claims.

1836 Inflation drives up the cost of living 66 percent.

The wealthy build summer houses in the Bronx countryside. As the New York & Harlem Rail Road is extended out from the City, small towns will grow up at station stops: Melrose, Morrisania, Tremont, Williamsbridge.

1836 The Astor House opens. Fashionable people who live in the country can now stay in town in style.

1837 The Panic causes a run on the banks. Foreclosures make John Jacob Astor very rich. Ten thousand people become dependent on almshouses, which can't cope, so many poor starve to death.

Ruins after the Great Fire of 1835

John Jacob Astor

The reading room at the Astor House hotel

1838 "Abandon hope, all ye who enter here." One hundred fifty male and fifty female criminals can be imprisoned in the Tombs, a massive new jail named for its Egyptian design. Built on marshy landfill where the Collect Pond once was, the Tombs soon begins to sink.

1837 Hungry mobs riot for flour at the warehouses.

1837 Washington Irving speaks of "the almighty dollar."

1837 Tiffany & Company opens near City Hall as a Stationery and Fancy Goods Store with $1,000 borrowed from Charles L. Tiffany's father. The first week's profit is thirty-three cents.

1837 The artist-inventor Samuel F. B. Morse demonstrates the electric telegraph. By 1846 New York and Philadelphia communicate by dots and dashes. Soon the City is the U.S. telegraphy center.

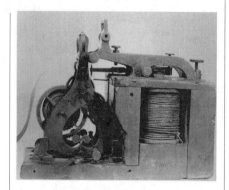

Telegraph recorder

1837 The five-story Old Brewery, built near the Collect Pond in 1792, has long been shut down, but staggering numbers of poor immigrants move in. Notorious for its Den of Thieves, the "rookery" is a hellhole without amenities.

1838 Frederick Douglass escapes to New York City from slavery in Maryland. The City is a center for abolitionism, but he is unsafe as a fugitive here, and moves to Massachusetts where he begins his work to free American blacks from bondage.

The Tombs

1840　The population of Manhattan is 312,710. A sixth of the island has houses, stores, and paved roads. The rest is gardens and farms.

Green-Wood Cemetery, Brooklyn

1840 Irish immigrant Bishop John Hughes asks the City to help the struggling Catholic schools, since the free schools are anti-Catholic. The City says no, and soon establishes the Board of Education. Hughes sets up the parochial school system; he also founds St. John's College, which will become Fordham University.

1840s The circus comes to town, one of many entertainments for working people. Others include variety and minstrel shows, melodramas, and panoramas.

Dime museums exhibit contortionists, fire and glass eaters, sword swallowers, fat and bearded ladies, freaks, snake charmers, two-headed calves, and four-legged chickens.

1841 A canal railroad system links the Hudson and Delaware Rivers, bringing Pennsylvania coal into City furnaces.

1841 John James Audubon buys a twenty-four-acre estate and wildlife preserve overlooking the Hudson at 155th Street.

Audubon's house

Croton Water celebration near City Hall

1842 Thousands of Irish immigrants in the Bronx, paid a dollar a day, complete the forty-one mile Croton Aqueduct, which brings clean Westchester water across High Bridge to the Reservoir on 42nd Street and Fifth Avenue. Thirty-five million gallons a day pour in. On the Fourth of July, the ecstatic City celebrates its new water supply with fireworks, fifty-foot high fountains, and parades. The aqueduct is one of the great engineering feats of the nineteenth century. By 1850 Croton cannot provide enough water for the growing City.

1842 The New York Philharmonic gives its first concert. In the German manner, all players stand but the cellists.

An Egyptian-style reservoir with a fashionable promenade around the top is built on the potter's field where 100,000 people have been buried. The New York Public Library with its great stone lions now stands on this spot.

1842 The world-famous author Charles Dickens arrives in New York City to begin a grand tour of the United States.

1843 P. T. Barnum exhibits Charles Stratton, a fifteen-pound, five-year-old child dwarf he presents as General Tom Thumb.

1844 Clipper ships—sleek, tall-masted vessels with undercut bows—sacrifice cargo space for speed. The finest are built in East River shipyards south of 13th Street, the hub of the City's dry docks.

1844 The Atlantic Avenue railroad tunnel in Brooklyn is built by Irishmen using the cut-and-cover method, which will be used for the subway system sixty years later. The tunnel is half a mile of bluestone and beautiful brickwork. Today the once-lost tunnel can be visited via a manhole at Atlantic and Court. Inside, the silence is profound.

1844 Black Master Juba beats white Master Diamond in a tap dance competition. Tap is a homegrown product of the Five Points, where African dances meet Irish jigs and clog dancing.

1844 The poet and *New York Evening Post* editor William Cullen Bryant calls for a central park because the island is being eaten up by commerce, with little space for health and recreation.

1845 Margaret Fuller, ardent feminist, becomes the first literary critic for the *New York Tribune*, then its foreign correspondent reporting on the Italian Revolution of 1848.

Tom Thumb's wedding in 1863 by Currier & Ives

Philanthropic organizations, such as the Association for Improving the Condition of the Poor, help to settle the increasing numbers of immigrants. Tammany Hall staves off despair with food baskets, jobs, shelter, and citizenship papers.

The Crystal Palace and reservoir at 42nd Street, 1855 (image reversed)

The Five Points

1845 A brilliant, eccentric writer publishes a poem about a large ebony-plumed bird hovering in his doorway. Edgar Allan Poe's "Raven" was written in his home on what is now West 3rd Street.

1845 Only 91 of 13,000 black New Yorkers have the vote. The property requirements for blacks keep almost all of them from voting.

1845 The City sets up a new day-and-night police department of 800 men.

1845 Fire sweeps through downtown New York, destroying three hundred buildings and taking thirty lives.

1845 New Yorkers start the Knickerbocker Base Ball Club and write out the rules of an age-old game. "The New York Game" is played near Madison Square at 27th Street, and within twenty years replaces cricket as the national sport.

1846 Trinity Church's new building is consecrated, its 260-foot steeple the highest point in the City. This is the façade we see today at the end of Wall Street.

1846 A. T. Stewart builds a lavish dry goods emporium with some innovations: patrons browse on their own rather than with sales clerks, and prices replace bargaining. Its success attracts other dry goods stores. The neighborhood has been changing from residential to commercial. The Stewart building on Broadway, between Chambers and Reade Streets, is now a New York City Landmark.

1847 A free academy is called for by City-wide referendum. It eventually becomes City College of New York. Naysayers ask why on earth the City would need so many college graduates. The college quietly goes about its business, turning the poor into taxpayers and Nobel Prize winners.

1847 According to the City's first accurate immigration records, 2.5 million people pass through the port of New York in the next thirteen years; because of the potato famines, more than one million of them are Irish.

The police chief writes a *Rogue's Lexicon* of slang, or "flash." The Irish have given us pal, bender, blarney, chum, blow-out, lark, square, to sponge, and to kick the bucket. Also from this era: dive and flophouse, hooker, free lunch, city-scape, traffic jam, hooligan. What H. L. Mencken called "linguistic exubera-tion" Walt Whitman labeled "the blab of the pave."

The new Trinity Church

"Boss" Tweed

1848 The Church of St. Ann and the Holy Trinity in Brooklyn commissions 7,000 square feet of stained-glass windows—the first such windows in the U.S. For the next half century, New York's stained-glass makers are the best in the nation.

1849 Brooklyn City Hall opens for business. Brooklyn's great port gets going.

1849 "Workingmen! Shall Americans or English rule in this country?" screams a broadside handed out when English actor William Macready is chosen to play Macbeth at the elite Astor Place Opera House. At the May 10 performance, 10,000 rioters (including gangs) go wild and threaten to storm the theater. Police and militia open fire on the mob and more than twenty die.

1849 The People's Washing and Bathing Establishment opens on Mott Street. In summer the poor wash in the East River for free.

1849 Walter Hunt patents the safety pin, but needs money and sells the rights for $100. He was the first American inventor of the sewing machine, followed by Elias Howe, but I. M. Singer's marketing skills—and factories in lower Manhattan—will bring the machine into people's houses, and transform the City's garment industry, already bursting at the seams.

1848 William Magear "Boss" Tweed, New York City's own impresario of corruption, finds his way into City politics via the volunteer fire company system. In a year he is foreman of Company No. 6 and in 1851 a City alderman, then a U.S. congressman. He is soon an important member of Tammany Hall, rising through the ranks from brave to grand sachem, his position in 1863.

1848 John Jacob Astor dies the richest man in the country, having made a $20 million fortune in furs, shipping and, above all, Manhattan real estate, which he knew to buy early and hold on to.

Brooklyn City Hall

Astor Place Riot

1850 Thirty thousand people greet Jenny Lind, "the Swedish Nightingale," when she arrives in New York. She sings at Castle Garden, and on her two-year tour earns an unheard-of $1,000 a concert plus expenses in her contract with P. T. Barnum.

Jenny Lind at Castle Garden

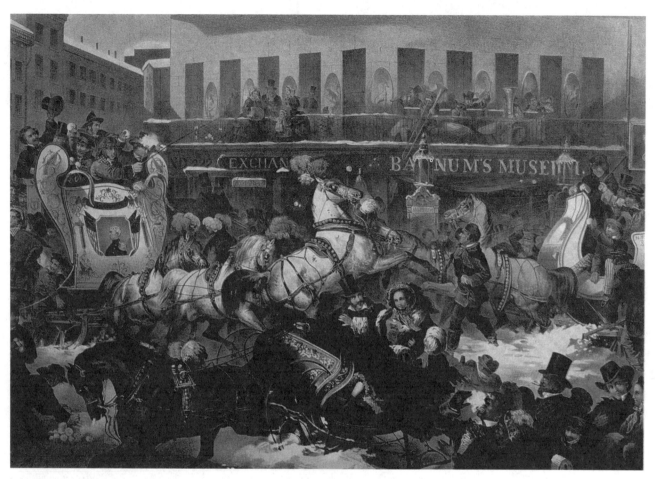

Broadway traffic, 1855

1850 New York City (Manhattan) population is 515,547.

Traffic makes a deafening roar at Broadway and Fulton Street, where 15,000 vehicles rattle and rumble by on any weekday. Jams are a regular event and a relief to pedestrians, who can cross the street safely through stalled traffic.

1850 Eight pairs of English sparrows are imported by the Brooklyn Institute to take care of a caterpillar problem in its shade trees.

1850 A survey finds 6,000 gaming houses in the City. As much as a twentieth of the City's inhabitants gamble to try to make ends meet.

1850 Two or three dollars a month is charged for an airless, lightless Lower East Side room in a new form of housing called the tenement. In Gotham Court, the first substandard housing built for the desperately poor, the few privies are in a grating-covered cellar under the alley.

1850 The "battle of the hatters," between small firms who make silk and beaver top hats for men, rocks this highly competitive business. In the 1890s the Knox Hat Company runs large factories in Brooklyn and sells hats in the United States, South America, and Europe.

1850 Five thousand people rally to celebrate the return to the City of a former slave, James Hamlet. He was captured in Brooklyn and sent to Baltimore under the Fugitive Slave Act; the New York Vigilance Committee has bought him back for $800.

1850 Archbishop John Hughes vows to build an extraordinary church on a piece of land at 50th Street and Fifth Avenue, despite the Protestant, anti-Catholic elite of the City. St. Patrick's Cathedral begins construction in 1859.

1851 *The New York Times* puts out its first issue.

1851 Harper's publishes Herman Melville's *Moby-Dick, or The Whale*. First printing: 2,915 copies. "Circumambulate the city of a dreamy Sabbath afternoon. Go from Corlear's Hook to Coenties Slip, and from thence, by Whitehall, northward. What do you see?—Posted like silent sentinels all around the town, stand thousands upon thousands of mortal men fixed in ocean reveries."

1852 The City builds seventy miles of sewers when wealthy homeowners complain that the new Croton system has raised the water table and their basements are flooding.

1853 Drovers are banned from herding cattle to the slaughterhouse through streets south of 42nd during daylight hours.

1853 Steinweg and sons open a piano factory. Their Steinway grand becomes world-famous.

May 1 is traditional moving day for tenants in the City, who each year try to improve their housing. Stores shut down for the day because streets are clogged with carts loaded with belongings.

1853 The first American World's Fair is held in Bryant Park. A spectacular domed iron-and-glass exhibition hall, the Crystal Palace is allegedly fireproof but five years later it burns down in fifteen minutes.

1853 In one Crystal Palace exhibition, Elisha Graves Otis demonstrates his steam-powered passenger elevator. Together with cheaper steel, writes historian James Trager, the elevator will lead "to the rise of the modern city."

1853 "I would prefer not to," says a forlorn legal secretary, so persistently refusing to do his work that he is locked up and dies in the Tombs, in Herman Melville's Wall Street story "Bartleby the Scrivener." It appears in *Putnam's Magazine*, a new monthly that

Building St. Patrick's Cathedral, 1868

The Crystal Palace

Crystal Palace interior

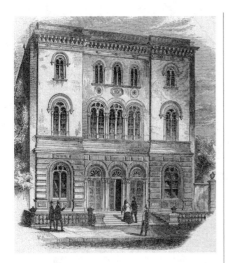

The Astor Library

boldly publishes American rather than British writers and folds after four illustrious years.

1854 Extra! Extra! Orphaned newsboys can get lodging for six cents a night at the nation's first Newsboys' Lodging House. Horatio Alger will write about these boys. (See 1868)

1854 The Astor Library opens on Lafayette Street in a building that is transformed in the 1960s into Joseph Papp's Public Theater.

1855 Castle Garden becomes the immigration station and receives a flood of immigrants until 1890. Built as Castle Clinton in 1811, the red sandstone fort was part of the City's defense during the War of 1812. It stood 300 feet off the tip of Manhattan until landfill attached it to the island. From 1826 to 1853 it was a profitable 5,000-seat theater. Today visitors buy tickets to Ellis Island and the Statue of Liberty there.

1855 A model tenement is tried at Mott and Elizabeth Streets, but few landlords are interested in improvements that would sharply cut their profits.

1855 Women's Hospital opens as the first institution in the world established by women for lying-in and for women's diseases. Nearly a hundred years later the hospital merges with St. Luke's at 114th Street and Amsterdam Avenue.

Immigrants landing at the Battery about 1847. Castle Garden is at left. Nearby is the junk Keying, the first Chinese ship in New York

Bird's-Eye View of New York and Brooklyn, 1850

1855 Walt Whitman self-publishes his *Leaves of Grass*. A Brooklyn booster for much of his life, he is journalist, writer, printer, and editor as well as poet (and a nurse in the Civil War). He writes that New York City is "the great place . . . the heart, the brain, the focus . . . the no more beyond of the western world."

1857 Elizabeth Blackwell, the first woman in the U.S. to receive a medical degree (1849), founds the New York Infirmary for Indigent Women and Children, run entirely by women, where female doctors can get clinical experience they cannot get elsewhere.

Walt Whitman

Elizabeth Blackwell

1857 Central Park (eventually 843 acres) is underway. It takes twenty years to complete, and in the process, established communities like Seneca Village are razed, churches removed, and 1,600 people dislocated. It is the first landscaped park in the nation and helps real estate investors sell the City. Most of the City's downtown poor cannot afford the fare to get there.

༝

A plant survey of the newly acquired land lists 280 species native to the region, from oaks to wild roses: 9,000 red maple, 8,000 oak, 3,000 black locust, and 300 flowering dogwood.

1857 To break Mayor Fernando Wood's grip on the City, the state creates a new police force, the Metropolitans, but Wood refuses to knuckle under. He names his police the Municipals, and the two forces battle it out at City Hall before the state court gets him to back down.

1857 Currier & Ives lithographs are published and sell for five cents to one dollar.

1857 The Panic of 1857 spreads through the nation. The country's manufacturing center is hard hit. Critical shortages of work and food drive the unemployed to protest, and the militia is called out against unruly mobs. Twenty banks and 10,000 businesses fail. Work on Central Park is given to the needy and paid for by the City.

1857 U.S. cities like New York have the highest death rate in the world because of poverty and overcrowding. Tuberculosis, which is not thought to be infectious, and intestinal diseases in children account for the vast majority of deaths in the City.

1858 R. H. Macy, a Nantucket Quaker who has given up whaling, comes to New York and opens a small store on 14th Street. The store moves to Broadway and 34th Street in 1902.

Wall Street, the Panic of 1857

55

1859 Newcomers get a rough start in the City. Half of those singled out for arrest this year are Irish. But 27 percent of the policemen are born in Ireland, too.

1859 Knickers becomes the new name for knee-length pants when Washington Irving's *Knickerbocker History of New York* is published with new illustrations.

1859 Cooper Union for the Advancement of Arts and Sciences opens to provide tuition-free classes for the poor. Its founder, Peter Cooper, is an inspired inventor, entrepreneur, and civic reformer. He runs for president in 1876 at the age of eighty-five.

1860 The City of Brooklyn assembles land for Prospect Park, today a spread of 526 acres.

1860 The first-ever dime novel, *Maleska: The Indian Wife of the White Hunter* by Anne S. W. Stephens, is published in New York.

1860 Nine U.S. cities have a population of more than 100,000: New York has 813,669; Brooklyn, still a separate city, has 279,122.

Half of Manhattan's people are foreign-born; about 204,000 from Ireland, and 120,000 from Germany. About 1 1/2 percent of Manhattan's residents are black, 12,500 people.

1860 Slavery is the subject of Abraham Lincoln's eloquent address in February to fifteen hundred people in the Great Hall at Cooper Union. In November he is elected president, and the following month South Carolina secedes from the Union.

1860 The cotton trade brings New York City $200 million a year. The City's merchants, worried about their cotton investments, side with the South.

1861 Mayor Fernando Wood suggests to the City Council that New York City secede from New York State to show its loyalty to the South and protect its own interests.

1861 The Civil War begins on April 12 and the people of New York City pledge loyalty to the Union. The biggest rally ever jams Union Square, and the City is decked with red, white, and blue bunting.

1861 New Yorkers raise $150 million for the Union in three months and provide more volunteers to the army than any other city. The wealthy underwrite loans to the federal government, and defense contracts bring profits to shipyards and machine shops.

1861 *The Tribune* calls New York southern sympathizers "copperheads."

1861 A circular addressed to "The Women of New York" brings in 4,000 women—including Astors, Roosevelts, and Coopers—to support the war effort and form the Women's Central Association of Relief, which helps provide medical supplies for the wounded.

Valley Grove Tavern in Prospect Park, 1876

Soldiers going to War

1861 The ironclad *Monitor* is built at Greenpoint, Brooklyn, and readied for battle. In 1862 she defeats the Confederate ironclad frigate *Merrimac* off the Virginia coast.

1863 The Draft Riots. Wartime hardship, anxiety over jobs lost to southerners, especially blacks, and federal conscription that allows the well-off to buy out for $300, drive the Irish working poor into the most violent urban rioting in national history. One hundred twenty-five people die; blacks are brutally beaten and lynched, and the Colored Orphan Asylum is torched. Policemen and City leaders are attacked. Five Union Army regiments are called from Gettysburg to restore order.

The Irish believe the blacks are taking their jobs away from them, but actually it is the other way around, notes the historian Ernest A. McKay.

1863 Metropolitan Life Insurance has its beginnings in the National Life & Limb Insurance Company.

1863 New four-wheeled roller skates allow for fancy footwork.

1864 Madame Restell, the preeminent abortionist, flaunts her success with her elegant five-story mansion on Fifth Avenue and 52nd Street.

1864 The songwriter Stephen Foster dies a poor man at Bellevue Hospital a few days after writing "Beautiful Dreamer."

The Draft Riots

Madame Restell's Fifth Avenue mansion

1865 Paid and uniformed firefighters replace the old volunteer system as New York and Brooklyn come under the jurisdiction of the Metropolitan Fire District.

A Guide to the Seraglios of New York lists tony bordellos for the upper crust, like the Seven Sisters on 27th Street.

1865 On April 9 New York City celebrates the end of the Civil War with bunting, cannon fire, and the singing of a grand "Te Deum" at Trinity Church. Not a week later the City is plunged into mourning at the news of the assassination of President Lincoln, whose funeral cortege arrives on April 24. Five hundred thousand mourners line the streets. The City is draped in black bombazine.

1865 Winslow Homer returns from the Civil War to make his name with war paintings.

1865 A volunteer corps of sanitary inspectors undertakes a massive block-by-block sanitation investigation of the epidemics devastating the City. In the Fourth District (south of Chatham Square), they find desperate overcrowding. An example: seventy-eight people sharing one privy.

1866 Cholera returns. The scourge has killed more than ten thousand New Yorkers in a few decades. The first municipal Board of Health in the country is created and given extensive powers.

1866 The first Broadway musical, the Faustian *Black Crook*, opens with a five-hour performance that includes 100 dancing girls in pink tights; it runs in New York for 474 performances and tours for forty years.

1867 The City's tenements are seen as breeding grounds for disease and crime. The state legislature responds with the first Tenement House Law in the nation, but despite the regulations, conditions get worse.

1867 A Brooklyn pitcher, William Arthur Cummings, throws the first curve ball.

1868 The new, extravagant Tammany Hall on 14th Street hosts the Democratic National Convention on July 4.

1868 Horse-drawn streetcars get caught in gridlock, so tracks start going up thirty feet in the air on Greenwich Street, then on Third, Sixth, and Second Avenues. The elevated trains soon run by steam. The noise is terrible; engines spew ash, oil, and cinders; buildings shake; and people's lives are cast into shadow. The system is the first rapid transit in the nation. In 1921, the peak year for the els, there are 384 million riders.

Lincoln's funeral cortege

1868 Horatio Alger publishes *Ragged Dick, or Street Life in New York*, the first of his 103 very popular rags-to-riches inspirational novels for boys.

1869 Sadie the Goat, gangleader, wears her chewed-off ear in a locket. She and her gang steal a sloop and turn pirate, making Hudson River captives walk the plank, writes Luc Sante in his 1991 book, *Low Life*.

1869 On Black Friday, September 24, the stock market crashes when robber barons Jay Gould and James Fisk try to corner the gold market.

The first elevated on Greenwich Street

The new Tammany Hall

1869 Hunter College is founded as the Female Normal and High School. It will train great numbers of teachers for the public schools. For the first time in the City, girls can get a free high school education.

1869 The American Museum of Natural History opens at the arsenal in Central Park but moves to its present site on Central Park West in 1877. Today it is going through a multimillion dollar renovation. Its exhibition halls display one of the best vertebrate fossil collections in the world.

1870 An underground pneumatic subway car is tested on 100 yards of track under Broadway, and 400,000 riders try it out. The tunnel was dug secretly by an entrepreneur because Boss Tweed, who gets a kickback from horse-drawn streetcars, sees a subway as a threat to his empire.

1870 Freight cars from the Pacific Coast arrive in New York, completing the first transcontinental freight rail connection.

1870 A new luxury apartment house on East 18th Street is modeled on buildings in Paris; it is five stories high, and has a concierge but no elevator. The six-room "French flats" with bath rent for $1,000 to $1,500 a year, but will gentlemen want to live in apartments?

1870 Eugenio Maria de Hostos—Puerto Rican educator, writer, and reformer—moves to New York to continue fighting for the liberation of Puerto Rico from Spain. In 1968 a branch of City University in the Bronx is named after him.

1871 J. P. Morgan organizes a new banking house, Drexel, Morgan & Co.

1871 The ferryboat SS *Westfield* explodes because of a rotten boiler, killing 104. By this time 50 million people a year ride the ferries across the East River.

1871 Ebenezer Butterick's dressmaking patterns come in a range of sizes, and his 12,500 styles make fitted clothing available for a whole class of women who cannot afford custom-made clothes.

1871 "The Greatest Show on Earth," P. T. Barnum's Circus, arrives in Brooklyn.

Beach's pneumatic subway

1871 Central Park's carousel, turned by a mule in a basement beneath the platform, gives adults and children their first ride. Today's carousel, brought from Coney Island when its predecessor burned, dates from 1908.

1871 The Tweed Ring, up to its usual shenanigans, has the City appropriate $13 million for the Tweed Courthouse, which is supposed to cost $250,000. One bill for a month's work by a carpenter comes to $361,000. The Courthouse, finished in 1878 behind City Hall, is today a landmark.

1871 Tweed faces his nemesis in Thomas Nast, who exposes the Boss in cartoons in *Harper's Weekly*. The *Times* follows suit with accounts of the crimes of the Tweed Ring. Mass meetings and his arrest and trials complete the job of bringing Tweed down, and the man who, with his cronies, stole $5 million to $200 million through graft and extortion is jailed. Released after a year, he is reconvicted on civil charges. He escapes but is brought back and dies in prison in 1878.

1871 Thomas Nast creates the donkey and elephant symbols for the Democratic and Republican parties.

1872 The spiritualist Victoria Woodhull is the first woman to run for president. With the backing of Cornelius Vanderbilt, she has made a fortune in her Wall Street brokerage firm, the first run by a woman.

1872 On Staten Island licorice-flavored chewing gum, Blackjack, is made by photographer Thomas Adams, who will also sell his new Tutti-Frutti gum from vending machines on elevated train platforms.

Fashion in Central Park

Thomas Nast's symbol for the Democratic Party

1873 Panic and financial disaster close the New York Stock Exchange for ten days. Five thousand businesses fail by year's end, and charities feed tens of thousands.

1874 Kingsbridge, Morrisania, and West Farms in Westchester are annexed to the City of New York, the first additions to the City since 1731.

1874 Hundreds of unemployed workers are injured at a meeting in Tompkins Square when they are charged by mounted police.

1874 The American Society for the Prevention of Cruelty to Animals takes pity on an abused and starving eight-year-old girl, and the American Society for Prevention of Cruelty to Children is founded.

1874 Macy's fills its first Christmas windows with dolls.

1874 Madison Square, named after James Madison, is a grand, fashionable park on 26th Street. P. T. Barnum's Great Roman Hippodrome opens on the park this year. The Hippodrome soon becomes Gilmore's Garden, site of beauty contests, temperance meetings, and dog shows. In 1879 William Vanderbilt builds Madison Square Garden on the site.

1875 Train tracks at street level on Park Avenue are sunk into a trench for safety and quiet.

The Grecian Bend

Heavy hoopskirts requiring twenty-five yards of material per dress are going out of style and the bustle is coming in.

1876 Boom! The reefs at Hell Gate are blasted away with dynamite, and the turbulent channel between Wards Island and Astoria, Queens, is cleared.

Train tracks covered over on Park Avenue

63

The Port of New York, 1878

1876 Fire breaks out during a performance of *The Two Orphans* at the Brooklyn Theatre, and 295 patrons die, many piled at the exits. New fire regulations for theaters call for exit doors to open outward.

1877 The world's first typing course, given at the YMCA, is for women. By the end of the century, women hold half the office jobs.

1877 The Fresh Air Fund is started for the poor children of the City. By the late 1990s, more than 1.6 million children have had country vacations arranged by the fund.

1877 Bell Telephone starts offering its telephones to the City. The public is soon outraged by the number of poles and the density of overhead telegraph and telephone wires.

1877 A Brooklyn businessman, Alfred Tredway White, pioneers cottages for workers, each with six rooms and renting for fourteen dollars a month.

1879 A competition produces the dumbbell plan for tenements, with a narrow air shaft and miserly layout. ("Dumbbell" refers to the floor plan of the buildings.) Reformers complain bitterly, but the plan is sanctioned by this year's Tenement House Law.

1879 In Brooklyn milk is now delivered in glass bottles. It used to be ladled into the residents' own containers from barrels stacked on a wagon.

1879 St. Patrick's, the twin-spired Gothic cathedral on Fifth Avenue, is dedicated. Construction has taken twenty years because of the war and has cost $1.9 million.

1879 Harrigan and Hart, the favorite Irish vaudeville team, use their Mulligan sketches to portray life in New York.

1879 The Ninth Avenue el expands northward from 59th Street, creating a new neighborhood, the Upper West Side.

Broadway north of 59th Street is called the Boulevard. A double row of elms shades the grassy mall in the center of the great thoroughfare, which is modeled on European boulevards to entice builders of grand mansions. The mansions go up elsewhere, however. In 1899 the avenue is renamed Broadway, and starting in 1901, digging for the subway tears up the graceful old street.

1879   The Tenderloin, also known as Satan's Circus, is the place to go for drinking, gambling, opium, and prostitution. From 24th to 40th Street, Fifth to Seventh Avenue, the Tenderloin is the best cut for bribes to the police.

1880   The English Muffin is introduced by Samuel Bath Thomas, whose bakery on 20th Street and 9th Avenue in Manhattan supplies hotels and restaurants by pushcart.

The rich and poor flood in . . .

The wealthy gravitate to New York. "The pattern was already established by the early eighties. By 1883 John D. Rockefeller and Collis P. Huntington had followed Carnegie, as had Montana mining millionaire William A. Clark, and many others." By 1892 the City is home to 1,265 millionaires. —Historian David C. Hammack

The poor gravitate to New York. They come from southern and eastern Europe, from Italy, Russia, and the Balkans. The Lower East Side is the most densely populated place on earth. Half of New York's residents are packed into tenements there. The area accounts for 70 percent of the City's deaths.

1880   The Metropolitan Museum of Art, today the nation's richest art museum, opens on Fifth Avenue in a new red-brick building. From the start the museum is dedicated to bringing art to the people through its outreach programs.

1880   Another grand red-brick building goes up to house the Brooklyn Historical Society on Pierrepont Street.

1880   Sarah Bernhardt, "the greatest tragic actress of the age," makes her New York debut at Booth's Theatre.

1880   *The New York Daily Graphic* prints the first newspaper photograph, a picture of a local shantytown.

1880   Cleopatra's Needle (1475 B.C.), a gift to the U.S. from the khedive of Egypt, is

shipped in sections to Staten Island, transferred to pontoons, and then rolled on cannonballs from the Hudson shore to Central Park, where the obelisk stands seventy feet high.

1881   The City runs out of water in a drought.

1882   P. T. Barnum brings Jumbo the elephant from England and parades him through City streets.

1882   Thomas Edison's giant steam-driven dynamos on Pearl Street—the first electrical generating plant in the world—light 7,200 lamps in the Wall Street area.

1882   Water supplies only 2 percent of houses; most private houses have a privy in the backyard. Tenements might have one faucet per floor.

Italian immigrants at Mulberry Bend, 1895

Hester Street market

1883 The Brooklyn Bridge, one of the wonders of the world, opens after fourteen years of construction and the loss of at least twenty-six lives. The new bridge connects Manhattan and Brooklyn, the first and third largest cities in the nation. The bridge builder, John Augustus Roebling, dies early in the construction. His son takes over as director, but gets Caissons disease, so his wife Emily helps complete the job.

1883 New York's new high society builds its own opera house, the 3,700-seat Metropolitan, at 39th Street and Broadway, because the old guard at the 14th Street Academy of Music has claimed all the best seats. The Met opens with Gounod's *Faust*.

1883 Mrs. William Vanderbilt, wife of the railroad magnate, planning to move up in society, gives a $250,000 fancy dress ball, the most extravagant to date, and spends $11,000 on flowers, $65,270 on food, and $155,730 on costumes.

1884 An earthquake, like the one in 1737, registers 5.0 on the Richter scale and is centered in Rockaway.

1884 Open-air treatment for tuberculosis is pioneered by a New York doctor who has recovered from the disease himself.

1884 The Dakota, a large and elegant apartment house, named after a distant American territory, opens at 72nd Street and Central Park West.

The Dakota, 1890

The Brooklyn Bridge celebration

1885 Businessmen lunching at the Exchange Buffet eat at the first self-service restaurant in the world.

1886 Honest John Kelly ends his tenure as the first Irish Catholic boss of Tammany Hall. As Master of Manhattan, the former New York alderman, congressman, sheriff, and comptroller has transformed Tammany into a modern political machine.

1886 Bartholdi's statue of "Liberty Enlightening the World" is dedicated on Bedloe's Island. A gift from the French, she presides over New York Harbor.

1886 The nation's first settlement house opens on the Lower East Side, and many more soon follow. These institutions are lifelines for the poor. They give immigrants shelter, medical care, classes, plays, clubs, and music. Settlement workers prod public officials for desperately needed reforms.

1886 Samuel Gompers, a cigar-maker who was born in London, becomes president of the American Federation of Labor, which he founded. Gompers calls the City "the cradle of the American labor movement."

1886 Bloomingdale's, opened in 1872 as the "great East Side store," moves to a site near the Third Avenue el at 49th Street to take advantage of middle-class customers who use the elevated line.

1886 "Avon Calling." A Brooklyn door-to-door book salesman starts the business that will grow into the world's biggest cosmetic company.

1886 Streetcar drivers strike for two dollars for a twelve-hour day with a half-hour break. In the next few years, the City's horse-drawn streetcars begin to be replaced with street cars drawn by cables, except on Fifth Avenue, where horses hold out until 1907.

1888 Pastrami on rye is served for the first time in a New York delicatessen. The Rumanian recipe for preserving beef falls into the hands of a miller-tinker-peddler-butcher, who finds riches between two slices of rye. But you can't eat the sandwich without sours or half-sours.

Inside the Statue of Liberty

1888 The Great Blizzard dumps twenty-one inches of snow and roars through town, pulling down telephone poles and cables. Telephone service is disrupted for two months. A new directive requires all overhead wires to be buried.

The Great Blizzard

After the Blizzard

1889 Mother Cabrini, a missionary nun and the first U.S. citizen to be canonized, is sent to New York City by Pope Leo XIII to aid Italian immigrants.

1889 The new Barnard College, affiliated with Columbia College, awards women the Bachelor of Arts degree. Columbia University moves into its classical buildings in the new Morningside Heights campus in 1897 and Barnard into its first building across Broadway in 1900.

1889 *The Wall Street Journal* summarizes financial news for two cents a copy and will have one of the largest circulations in the country.

1889 The Harlem Opera House, built by Oscar Hammerstein on 125th Street, opens in anticipation of a fashionable Harlem.

1889 The *New York World* reporter Elizabeth "Nellie Bly" Cochrane, age twenty-two, leaves Hoboken on November 14 on assignment to travel around the world in less than Jules Verne's eighty days. Faster than Phileas Fogg, she arrives back in New Jersey on January 25 in 72 days.

1890 One million people live in 37,316 tenement houses.

1890 Eighty percent of the City's population has foreign-born parents.

1890 Stanford White's new Madison Square Garden on 26th Street draws 17,000 on opening night. The horse show arena has a theater, a roof garden, and a spectacular tower.

1890 The photographer and writer Jacob Riis, an immigrant from Denmark, publishes his study of New York City's poor, *How the Other Half Lives*. Riis takes pictures in dark tenements with a new flash powder and wakes up the City.

1891 The New Croton Aqueduct opens, providing the City with 300 million gallons of water a day. The original Croton Aqueduct, phenomenal in 1842, is outdated. In the late 1990s the path along the original Aqueduct is a walker's delight.

1891 Cedar water tanks perched on top of buildings become part of the City skyline. By the 1990s there are 10,000 of them.

1891 Herman Melville dies in obscurity. He has lived near Madison Square for twenty-eight years.

1891 Tchaikovsky conducts his work at the opening of Carnegie Hall on West 57th Street.

1892 Corruption has ended Castle Garden's role as New York's immigration station. The feds take over and Ellis Island becomes the U.S. Immigration Center. It screens half a million to a million arrivals a year; 98 percent are admitted.

"Eugene Schieffelin, a member of an old and wealthy New York family, released eighty starlings in Central Park, so New Yorkers could see the birds mentioned in Shakespeare's plays. Today, their 200 million descendants fill the skies across America," write Roy Rosenzweig and Elizabeth Blackmar in 1992.

Ellis Island

1892 The episcopal Cathedral Church of St. John the Divine, planned as the world's largest cathedral, has its cornerstone set. In the tradition of the great medieval cathedrals, it will take more than a century to build and is still not finished today.

1893 The stock market crashes on June 27, and the nation suffers a four-year depression.

1893 The New York City inventor Thomas Edison markets his electrically driven peephole viewer, the kinetoscope, intended to entertain one person at a time.

1893 The Russian-American anarchist Emma Goldman sets up hunger demonstrations during the devastating depression and tells 3,000 people in Union Square that if they can't afford to buy bread they should take it.

1893 The Municipal Art Society is started by citizens concerned about public art in the City. Ten years later the society is planting trees on Brooklyn streets, suggesting a whole new look for the City. Today it's an advocate for landmark preservation.

1893 Louis Comfort Tiffany's art nouveau lamps are fashioned in Corona, Queens, from metalwork and favrile, his patented, variegated glass. Tiffany's designs display flowers, birds, and dragonflies in myriad colors.

Henry Street Settlement Visiting Nurse, 1908
A short cut over the roofs of the tenements
by Jessie Tarbox Beals

1893 Hog Island, with its pavilions and bathing huts, is destroyed by the hurricane that floods lower Manhattan and uproots 100 trees in Central Park. This barrier island off the Rockaways, which appeared at the time of the Civil War, sinks back into the sea in 1902 after a series of storms.

1893 The bandleader John Philip Sousa moves into his studio at the top of Carnegie Hall. His "Manhattan Beach March" celebrates an elegant new Brooklyn resort.

1894 Who wants to ride in a hole in the ground? New Yorkers do. An ambitious subway system is voted in. It will become the largest rapid transit system in the world.

1894 The state senate's Lexow Committee brings charges against sixty-seven City policemen for vice operations, election rigging, and brutality. As a result, Tammany Hall loses the mayoral election, but it takes control of New York again three years later.

Ah there! Coney Island

1895 Theodore Roosevelt, the new Police Board president, plunges into cleaning up police corruption.

1895 Stanford White's Washington Memorial Arch replaces a wooden arch erected to commemorate the centennial of George Washington's 1789 inauguration. Today the arch still marks the Fifth Avenue entrance to Washington Square Park.

1895 Lillian Wald and Mary Brewster open the Henry Street Settlement, the first organization to use visiting nurses. The service cares for thousands of patients in their homes and helps new mothers.

1895 The New York Public Library, created from the Astor and Lenox Libraries and the Tilden Trust, is free to the public.

1895 The great era of Coney Island begins with Sea Lion Park offering rides and amusements for masses of families.

1895 The country's first pizzeria opens on Spring Street.

1896 When the vitascope, an early movie projector, is demonstrated at a Broadway theater, the audience jumps up, afraid of getting soaked by the waves of Dover rolling in on the film. Thomas Edison claims many of the technical patents for filmmaking, and for the next two decades New York is the capital of the movie industry.

1896 Two-wheelers are the rage of the Gay Nineties, and Madison Square Garden's bicycle exhibition draws 120,000 spectators. A bike costs about a hundred dollars.

1896 Tootsie Rolls, paper-wrapped penny candies, are made by an Austrian-American, Leo Hirschfield, who calls them what he calls his daughter Clara.

1896 A New Yorker points out that the Constitution is color-blind. U.S. Supreme Court Judge John Harlan is the only judge to dissent when the Supreme Court upholds segregation in Plessy v. Ferguson.

1896 The New York Botanical Garden opens in the Bronx with contributions from the wealthiest people in the City. The Hemlock Grove is part of the last piece of original forest inside City limits today. Native evergreens (*Tsuga canadensis*) have stood there in majesty since Indians walked the land.

1896 The Dow Jones Industrial Index begins continuous publication. It averages stock prices of twelve companies.

1896 The world's first public golf course opens in Van Cortlandt Park.

1896 Tennessee newspaperman Adolph Ochs buys the failing *New York Times* and aims for journalistic respectability.

1896 Mills Hotel No. 1 on Bleecker Street discreetly offers tiny rooms—fifteen hundred of them—to poor men for twenty cents a night. Meals cost ten to twenty-five cents.

1896 Enough of the old-fashioned ward system of local school trustees. The City is struggling to accommodate massive numbers of immigrant children and puts trained professionals at the central Board of Education in charge. Full centralization of City schools follows in 1902.

1897 The *Jewish Daily Forward*, a Yiddish newspaper, runs its first issue.

1897 Grant's Tomb, at 122nd Street and Riverside Drive, the largest mausoleum in the United States, is modeled after the tombs of Mausolus, Hadrian, and Napoleon and dedicated on the general's birthday. The monument is renovated in 1997 in time for its centennial.

1897 A *New York Sun* editorial by a former Civil War correspondent assures a West 95th Street girl that "Yes, Virginia, there is a Santa Claus. He exists as certainly as love and generosity and devotion exist."

Sturgeon and shad are harvested from the great Hudson River, but pollution begins to threaten the industry.

Consolidation . . .

1897 Throughout the century, New York has been thinking big, building grand public works like the Erie Canal and the Croton Aqueduct. The civic leader Andrew Haswell Green and the Chamber of Commerce have worked for decades to bring over forty municipalities into one great consolidated city. On May 4 Green's dream is signed into reality by Governor Frank S. Black.

1898 January 1. Manhattan, Brooklyn, the Bronx, Queens, and Staten Island join together officially to become Greater New York, a city of five boroughs. Its population is 3.4 million, second only to London.

1898 Greater New York's harbor is the unifying concept behind the consolidation of the five boroughs—and it works. The port is the greatest in the world until the 1950s.

1898 A circulation war between William Randolph Hearst's *Journal* and Joseph Pulitzer's *World* heats up the country for the Spanish-American War; "yellow journalism" triumphs.

1898 Nikola Tesla, brilliant inventor, electrical engineer, showman, and threat to Edison, demonstrates the "Tesla coil," which contributes to the development of broadcasting. Tesla's discoveries include an arc lighting system and alternating-current transmission.

1899 The Bronx Zoo opens. Today a growing troupe of gorillas ponder the thousands of spectators gawking at them.

1899 "Dig We Must." Consolidated Edison results from the merger of Edison Illuminating Company with Consolidated Gas, owned by John D. Rockefeller and William Whitney.

Hospitals, orphanages, and settlement houses "did not represent mere benevolent impulse or humanitarian emotionalism; they reflected rather a hardheaded understanding that the cauldron of nationalities that was New York could survive only with a pattern of government and social action which recognized the humanity of each of the city's inhabitants." —Historian Milton M. Klein

---

Photographs record the vitality and tragedy of the burgeoning city. Jacob Riis, Lewis Hine, Alice Austen, Jessie Tarbox Beals, and the Byron Company create indelible images of people's lives.

1900   Broadway becomes the Great White Way when electric lights replace gas.

1900   The first U.S. National Automobile Show opens at Madison Square Garden. The ban on cars in Central Park has just been lifted and those noisy frightening playthings of the rich putter along the carriageways and destroy the quiet.

1900   Almost a quarter of the City is now German.

1900   The International Ladies Garment Workers Union (ILGWU) is started by cloakmakers determined to end the seventy-hour week and the treacherous sweatshop conditions.

1900   The Shubert brothers buck the existing Theatrical Syndicate to start building their own empire. Their organization remains one of the most powerful on and off Broadway.

1901   Streetcars are converted to electricity and become fast and dangerous.

1901   The steel magnate Andrew Carnegie gives money to build sixty-five public library branches throughout the City.

1901   83,000 tenements house 70 percent of the City's population in horrendous conditions. These "old law" buildings are declared substandard by a new Tenement House Law. "New law" buildings are a marked improvement.

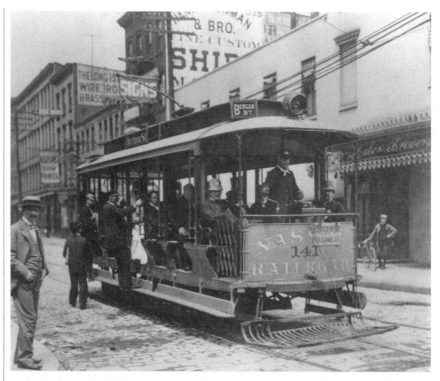

Electric trolley, Nassau Railroad

Andrew Carnegie, 1908

1902   The Fuller Building, known as the Flatiron for its shape on a little triangle of land, goes up twenty stories high—300 feet—at Broadway and Fifth.

1902   The teddy bear is born in Brooklyn to a Russian American candy store couple named Michtom, who manufacture the toy for a ready market. President Theodore Roosevelt okays the use of his nickname.

Teddy bear

The Flatiron Building

1902 The Algonquin Hotel opens on West 44th Street. The literati gather there during the 1920s to show off their sophisticated, acerbic style of humor to each other at Round Table discussions led by Alexander Woollcott, Harold Ross (later editor of *The New Yorker*), Dorothy Parker, and others.

1902 Muckraker Ida Tarbell's exposé of Standard Oil appears in installments in *McClure's*, one of the City's mass-circulation magazines for the middle class across America. *A History of the Standard Oil Company* shows that John D. Rockefeller controls virtually the entire U.S. oil refining industry, bringing him $45 million a year; the exposé leads to the Supreme Court's 1911 breakup of the company. In 1909 Rockefeller becomes the world's first billionaire.

1903 The tenor Enrico Caruso gives his first Metropolitan Opera performance, in *Rigoletto*.

1903 The Williamsburg Bridge opens Williamsburg, Brooklyn, once a fashionable German and Austrian enclave, to the poor of the Lower East Side. By 1920 this community has over a quarter of a million people packed into cold-water flats and tenements.

1903 When the pediatrician S. Josephine Baker breaks gender barriers to become the City's assistant health commissioner, her all-male staff resigns in protest, but her initiatives will cut the death rate in poverty-stricken neighborhoods by 80 percent, down to forty-three a day.

1904 The IRT (West Side Subway), operated by a rich New Yorker, August Belmont, runs its first train from City Hall to 145th Street via 42nd Street and then Broadway. The ride takes twenty-six minutes and costs five cents. The IRT will be the first underground system with both express and local tracks.

> Construction of the subway during the first thirty years of the century is an extraordinary feat. Thirty thousand men, many of them southern Italian immigrants who were squeezed off their land, dig the trench for the tracks. The work is done largely by hand, rather than with steam shovels, to avoid hitting the tangle of pipes and wire conduits already laid under the streets.

1904 Speculators gamble on the middle class moving uptown with the subway, but they don't come, so blacks can rent and buy the new, attractive row houses and apartments. Philip Payton, a black real estate developer in Harlem, encourages the City's black population to take advantage of adequate housing for the first time ever.

> A black congregation, St. Philip's Protestant Episcopal Church, soon buys ten new apartment houses on 135th Street and Lenox Avenue with the half million dollars it was paid for its holdings in the West 20s and 30s.

1904 Longacre Square is renamed Times Square when *The New York Times* moves up to 42nd Street at Seventh Avenue and Broadway, the new center of the City. Times Square is known as the crossroads of the world.

1904 The millionaire Joseph Pulitzer, a master at whipping up circulation and advertising in his newspapers, gives $16,500 to Columbia University to establish the Pulitzer Prize. He also endows the university's School of Journalism.

1904 Typhoid Mary, a carrier of the disease though not a victim herself, indirectly causes thirteen hundred cases of typhoid as a cook and kitchen worker. She continues to work under false names until 1915, when she is hospitalized for the rest of her life.

1904 The paddle steamer *General Slocum* catches fire in the East River and sinks on a church outing. More than 1,030 die, mostly women and children. The German community is devastated, and the heart of Kleindeutschland moves from Tompkins Square up to Yorkville.

1904 George M. Cohan's song "Give My Regards to Broadway" is first heard on Broadway.

The Times Building, 1904

1904 A Japanese exhibit at the New York Botanical Garden accidentally imports *Cryphonectria parasitica*, the blight that today is still destroying the American chestnut.

1904 The first tea bags appear when the merchant Thomas Sullivan packs sample teas in muslin bags and sends them to his customers.

1905 Richard Strauss's decadent opera *Salome* is banned at the Metropolitan until 1934.

1905 The Staten Island ferry is taken over by the City, and its five new boats are named after the five boroughs. The ride costs five cents until 1974.

1905 At nickelodeons (the new movie theaters) a nickel buys the latest entertainment: one-minute movies, ten-minute one-reelers, and boisterous honky-tonk.

Automatic vaudeville

1907 The era of the taxicab arrives. The slow, old hansom cabs powered by 800-pound batteries are replaced by gas-powered, taxi-metered vehicles. Within months 5,000 drivers strike for better wages and a union.

1907 J. P. Morgan brokers a deal to lend the City a desperately needed $30 million and saves it from financial panic during the national crisis.

1907 The United States Custom House is built in the Beaux Arts style on the site of the old Dutch fort of 1626. It faces Bowling Green, which has been kept an open space since the Dutch settled New Amsterdam.

1907 Rube Goldberg, later known for his zany contraptions, starts as a sports cartoonist for the *Evening Mail*.

1907 Florenz Ziegfeld's *Follies* bring class to vaudeville at 42nd Street's New Amsterdam Theater. The impresario puts his slim, long-legged women on the stage in twenty-one annual revues dedicated to the "glory of the American girl" and changes the image of the ideal woman. Plump is out.

1907 Society women, wanting a respectable place to stay in town, build the Colony Club, which is patterned after the most exclusive men's clubs.

J. P. Morgan

United States Custom House

1907 New York's most famous hotel, the Plaza, with 800 rooms, opens on Fifth Avenue and Central Park South.

1908 The subway goes under the East River to Brooklyn and over the Harlem River to the Bronx.

1908 "Take Me Out to the Ball Game" is a new song written by two New Yorkers.

1908 Brooklyn gets its own grand theater center, the Brooklyn Academy of Music. In the 1980s the Next Wave Festival makes it famous again.

1908 The Metropolitan Life Tower at 24th Street and Madison Avenue, modeled after the campanile in Venice's St. Mark's Square, is the tallest building in the world, at 700 feet, until the Woolworth Building tops it by 92 feet in 1913.

1908 The Sullivan Law requires restaurant owners to stop women from smoking in public.

BEGINNING MONDAY EVENING, SEPT. 13, 1909
Evenings at 8.15—Matinees Wednesday and Saturday at 2.15

WALKER WHITESIDE
In the New Play by Israel Zangwill
Treating of the amalgamation of the races in the making of the American

"THE MELTING POT"
LIEBLER & CO., Managers

1909 *The Melting Pot*, a crusading play by Israel Zangwill, coins the phrase in the place that epitomizes it.

1909 The Queensboro Bridge reaches across to the "suburbs." Soon the subway provides another link to Queens, and a European garden city movement suggests an alternative to dark, crowded tenement housing. America's first garden apartment cooperatives will go up beginning in 1917 in a new neighborhood named Jackson Heights.

1909 The City celebrates a double anniversary with the greatest naval parade ever seen in America. It's the 300th birthday of Henry Hudson's 1609 voyage and the 102nd birthday of Robert Fulton's 1807 first steamboat run. Replicas of the *Half Moon* and the *Clermont* take part.

1909 The first airplane to fly over New York Harbor is piloted by Wilbur Wright.

1909 The NAACP is founded by the writer and human rights activist W. E. B. Du Bois and liberals Jane Addams and John Dewey. Its headquarters remain in New York City until 1986.

1909 Teenage immigrant working girls lead the first mass women's strike in the country as 20,000 shirtwaist (blouse) makers walk out of Lower East Side sweatshops for three months. A judge accuses the women of striking against God.

1910 Mayor William J. Gaynor cleans the City's payroll of 400 no-shows and is shot by a discharged City dockworker. He continues as mayor but never really recovers his health.

1910 Excavating for Pennsylvania Station has been like digging the Panama Canal. The building is modeled after the Roman Baths of Caracalla but modernized with steel-ribbed interiors and a grand spectacle of glass domes and vaults. Trains run for the first time this year.

&

Vaudeville introduces Al Jolson, George Jessel, Sophie Tucker, Jack Benny, Groucho Marx, George Burns, Fanny Brice, and Eddie Cantor.

&

Melodies and piano music pouring and clattering out of windows on the West Side (first 28th, then 42nd, then 45th Street) earn those blocks and the popular music industry the name Tin Pan Alley. From the 1880s to the 1950s, Tin Pan Alley is the national capital of songwriters, publishers, and pluggers.

1910 The movie industry starts to leave New York City for the West Coast; the lure is good weather, cheap real estate, and freedom from the East Coast movie monopoly of Thomas Edison.

Mayor William J. Gaynor is shot

1910 *Women's Wear Daily* begins publication, and its owner, Edmund Fairchild, who started out as a peddler, builds a trade magazine publishing empire.

1911 The Triangle Shirtwaist Company fire kills 146 women trapped in the burning factory. Many leap to their deaths. Public outrage forces better working conditions for laborers.

1911 Two great stone lions by E. C. Potter preside over the entrance to the new, awe-inspiring New York Public Library at 42nd Street and Fifth Avenue.

1911 On one day in April, 11,745 immigrants pass the eye exam for trachoma and set an entry record at Ellis Island. Over the past 100 years 24 million immigrants have come through the Port of New York, the biggest population shift in the history of the world.

1911 "Alexander's Ragtime Band" combines styles of popular music to get feet tapping and makes a Tin Pan Alley name for its composer, Irving Berlin, the king of American songwriters.

> Irving Berlin (Israel Baline) learned to swim in the East River as a boy and often swims the turbulent, polluted water clean across to the Brooklyn shore.

> The *Autobiography of an Ex-Colored Man* by James Weldon Johnson gives whites a new glimpse of black culture. Johnson is a lawyer, poet, essayist, editor, teacher, leader. The song he wrote with his brother, "Lift Every Voice and Sing," comes to be known as the black national anthem. Johnson will serve as secretary of the NAACP for fifteen years.

1912 New York theaters are desegregated.

1912 The *Titanic* strikes an iceberg on its way to New York and the unsinkable sinks. More than fifteen hundred are lost, including the New York millionaires John Jacob Astor IV, Isidor Straus, and Benjamin Guggenheim.

1913 Grand Central Terminal replaces the old depot which can no longer cope with the volume of rail traffic. Sixty-seven tracks on two levels, and the vast marble palace, can handle 70,000 rail passengers an hour.

Irving Berlin

1913 The Woolworth Building, a graceful skyscraper, is finished. An awed visiting minister calls it a Cathedral of Commerce. The lobby is richly adorned with Ravenna mosaics in gold, blue, and red as well as sculpted caricatures of Frank Woolworth counting coins and architect Cass Gilbert holding a model of the building.

1913 Thirty-five thousand lingerie makers organized by Rose Schneiderman go on strike.

Rose Schneiderman

The lobby of the Woolworth Building

sent American painting, but viewers are far more shocked by the work of European artists like dadaist Marcel Duchamp.

1913 The Regent Theater, considered the world's first movie palace, is modeled on the Venetian Doge's Palace and seats eighteen hundred. Huge movie palaces are not meant to turn a profit. Film companies run them to inveigle the public into falling in love with the movies, which it does. (The Regent, now a church, stands at Adam Clayton Powell Jr. Boulevard and 116th Street.)

1913 Brooklyn's Ebbets Field ballpark opens. The Brooklyn Dodgers will get their name from Brooklynites known for their skill at dodging trolleys.

1913 Actors' Equity is founded.

1913 The Palace Theater at Broadway and 47th Street charges two dollars while other vaudeville houses charge fifty cents. Sarah Bernhardt, W. C. Fields, and Ed Wynn are worth the price of admission to the Palace.

1913 The Armory Show, held at the 69th Regiment Armory, introduces New York to modern art. Young, radical painters repre-

The Regent Theater on 116th Street

1913 Twenty columns adorn the solemn Classical Revival General Post Office building at Eighth Avenue between 32nd and 34th Streets, designed by McKim, Mead & White. Its inscription ("Neither snow, nor rain," etc.) adapts Herodotus' fifth-century B.C. words of praise for fleet-footed Persian messengers.

1913 *New York World* readers are puzzled by the first American crossword.

1914 The Municipal Building, whose arcade frames an entrance to Lower East Side slums, houses City offices as well as a chapel. Its wedding-cake tower is topped by Adolf Weinman's gilt figure, "Civic Fame,"

Dodgers-Giants National League season opener at Ebbets Field, Brooklyn

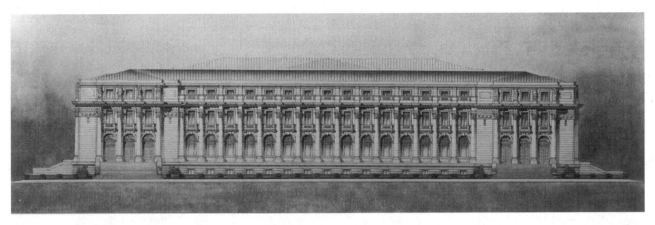

General Post Office Building

holding a crown with five points for the City's five boroughs.

1914 A debutante, Mary Phelps Jacob, who is a descendant of Robert Fulton, makes the first brassiere.

1914 On July 31 the New York Stock Exchange shuts down for six months because of World War I.

1914 Amalgamated Clothing Workers is a new union that does not look down its nose at immigrants and the poor who make men's clothing in dehumanizing sweatshops and dark tenements. This progressive union has broken away from the United Garment Workers and soon runs a bank, housing projects, and a health center for its members.

1914 On its opening day the Federal Reserve Bank of New York receives commercial bank deposits of over $99 million.

1914 The public schools are overwhelmed and turn away as many as 70,000 immigrant children a year.

1915 A new City flag is raised at City Hall to mark the 250th anniversary of the English takeover of New Amsterdam from the Dutch. The flag honors the Dutch with its background of blue, white, and orange; the seal in its center is an updated version of the original British one. The seal is displayed today on the NYPD badge.

1916 New zoning restrictions are demanded after the Equitable Building of 1915 takes a huge slice of sky from its neighbors on lower Broadway. It is forty stories high and a whole city block in bulk.

1916 During the City's worst poliomyelitis epidemic, more than 8,000 children under the age of ten are victims of the paralytic disease. The mortality rate for children is more than one in four. The City shuts down the-

aters and parks; public schools delay opening. In the 1950s polio is still a threat, and children are taught not to touch their mouths to water fountains.

1916 Nathan's famous frankfurter comes to Coney Island. Nathan and Ida Handwerker make the five-cent hot dog from a secret recipe and work eighteen hours a day at their food stand to undersell competitors.

1916 Brownsville, Brooklyn, has the first family-planning clinic in the world outside Holland. Margaret Sanger, who began as a visiting nurse on the Lower East Side and started the Brooklyn clinic, is arrested and sent to the Queens Penitentiary, where she lectures her fellow inmates on birth control.

> ❧
>
> American financiers block German transactions and support the Allies with offers of loans, even though the U.S. has not yet joined in the war.

1916 A huge explosion at the Black Tom, New Jersey, ammunition depot breaks windows in Brooklyn, peppers the Statue of Liberty with shell casings, and kills seven. World War I comes close to home for the City with this act of German sabotage.

1917 The U.S. enters World War I, providing the Allies unlimited manpower and matériel and raising morale at the front. Customs officers take over German ships in New York Harbor, the army posts soldiers on all the City's piers, and a steel net to stop U-boats is strung underwater across the Verrazano Narrows.

For the duration of the war, German opera is cut from the Metropolitan's repertory, hamburgers become "liberty sandwiches," and sauerkraut "liberty cabbage." Public schools suspend the teaching of German.

1917 The new Catskill Aqueduct brings water from 100 miles north of Manhattan. This huge engineering feat costs $277 million. The Croton Aqueduct system no longer has to do it alone.

1917 Hell Gate Bridge over the East River connects the mainland (the Bronx) with Queens and links New England by rail to the lower half of the northeast corridor (Philadelphia, Baltimore, Washington). The City is too dependent on this bridge for rail freight, and while barges regularly carry railway cars across the harbor, calls for a freight tunnel are heard.

1917 Fifteen thousand New York blacks led by W. E. B. Du Bois and James Weldon Johnson march in silence down Fifth Avenue to protest the massacre in East St. Louis, where a mob ran wild, killing blacks and burning them in their houses.

Hell Gate Bridge

1918 Influenza kills 12,000 New Yorkers and more than 20 million people worldwide.

1918 The jazz pianist and composer Fats Waller gets his start at a talent contest.

1918 Planes fly mail daily between New York and Washington, D.C. It's the first regular airmail route in the country.

1918 The worst accident in subway history kills 97 riders in Brooklyn and injures 250. The train, run by an inexperienced motorman during a strike, is traveling at 45 mph instead of 6 mph on a dangerous S curve under Malbone Street. The Brooklyn Rapid Transit goes bust, and the BMT takes over.

1918 The Bronx International Exposition of Science, Arts, and Industries, planned as a world's fair, has to be scaled back because of the war.

1919 New York City welcomes home soldiers from World War I.

1919 Roseland Ballroom opens. It's in a different class from seedy dance halls where men can buy a dance for a dime.

1919 The cost of living in New York City has increased 79 percent in five years.

1919 *The New York Daily News* is the first City tabloid. The paper is aimed at the Sweeneys, the masses, and leaves the Stuyvesants to take care of themselves.

1920 Babe Ruth, age twenty-four, joins the Yankees, purchased from the Boston Red Sox for $125,000. The Sultan of Swat hits 54 home runs in his first Yankee season.

1920s 32,000 speakeasies thrive in Prohibition-era New York. Rumrunners and bootleggers take advantage of the harbor and the waterfront to supply the nation, and organized crime gets a great boost.

1920 The Nineteenth Amendment gives women the right to vote. City women have organized for decades.

The End of the Climb

1920s Finally the City builds schools to accommodate the great numbers of immigrant children. Two hundred public schools go up in the decade's construction boom.

1920 After staggeringly high immigration, almost 30 percent of the City is Jewish.

1920s Harlem becomes a black neighborhood as 120,000 whites move out to new City neighborhoods and 120,000 blacks move in.

1920 Edith Wharton's *Age of Innocence*, which wins the Pulitzer Prize, describes 1870s upper-class New York in a state of denial. "There was something about the luxury of the Welland house and the density of the Welland atmosphere, so charged with minute observances and exactions, that always stole into his system like a narcotic. The heavy carpets, the watchful servants, the perpetually reminding tick of disciplined clocks. . . ."

1920 "Wise Men Fish Here." Frances Steloff opens the Gotham Book Mart, and it soon becomes the "New York writers' and readers' bookstore." It survives by the skin of its teeth today on West 47th Street.

1920 Music to the ears! Radio stations crank up to bring listeners music and other entertainments.

Afternoon shopping in Harlem, about 1944

Frances Steloff in 1963

1920 Prizefighting is legal again as long as it's supervised. Republican reformers are powerless to stop it. Madison Square Garden becomes the national venue for pugilism.

1921 New York and New Jersey have to share the harbor. They establish the Port of New York Authority and, amazingly, agree on guidelines.

1921 Vincent Sardi's restaurant opens on West 44th Street, where it remains today at the heart of the theater district.

1922 The Cotton Club opens in Harlem as a fashionable cabaret. Black customers are rarely allowed in, but black performers Duke

Ellington, Bill "Bojangles" Robinson, Stepin Fetchit, Lena Horne, Louis Armstrong, and Ethel Waters make the club's reputation.

1923 Paul Robeson, the son of a runaway slave, graduates from Columbia University Law School, but heads for a career as actor, great bass singer, and political activist. By 1940 he will be "the most famous black man in America."

1923 *Time* magazine is launched by Henry Luce. It summarizes the news, often as reported in *The New York Times*. The first issue costs fifteen cents.

1923 The Museum of the City of New York opens in Gracie Mansion. It is the nation's first city museum, with collections as vibrant and varied as the City itself. Its mis-sion, through exhibitions, education, and research, is to tell the remarkable story of New York from the Dutch period to the present. It will move to Fifth Avenue and 103rd Street in 1932.

1923 Yankee Stadium opens in the Bronx, and thousands of people are turned away for lack of seats. Babe Ruth hits a three-run homer. The Yankees win their first World Series.

The Museum of the City of New York

Prizefighting with Dempsey and O'Gatty

1923 Six-day bicycle races, the latest thing, are held at Madison Square Garden.

1923 The black vocalist Bessie Smith records "Down Hearted Blues" for Columbia Records. She sings the stories of southern blacks who migrate to northern cities, and her records go on to sell millions of copies.

1923 The Charleston comes to New York in *Runnin' Wild*, a black revue on Broadway, and becomes the dance of the decade.

87

The Sixth Avenue el about 1938

1923 The Lebanese poet Kahlil Gibran, since 1911 a New Yorker living on West 10th Street, publishes *The Prophet*, which will sell more than 8.5 million copies.

1923 The City starts the long process of dismantling its old elevated railways. Manhattan's last el, the Third Avenue, is demolished in 1955. Some el tracks are rebuilt to be a part of the subway system, but a decrepit unreconstructed el carries Brooklyn's Franklin Avenue Shuttle until 1998, when renovation will finally begin.

1923 Mayor Hylan starts building a railroad tunnel between Brooklyn and Staten Island to give freight carriers another way, besides Hell Gate Bridge, into New York City. The Port Authority says the rail link is necessary. Hylan and the tunnel are stopped for political reasons, and Jimmy Walker is nominated to be the next mayor. The freight tunnel was never completed. (See 1998)

1924 New York's open door for the huddled masses slams shut with the federal National Origins Act, which sharply restricts immigration. The quota system favors "Nordic" people from the United Kingdom and Germany.

1924 Louis Armstrong moves here as the country's jazz center shifts from Chicago to New York. Unlike Chicago, New York doesn't take Prohibition seriously, and it cuts records, makes broadcasts, and likes newcomers.

1923 Martha Graham moves to the City and develops modern dance. New York is soon the world's modern dance center.

1923 A Russian immigrant, Ida Rosenthal, designs a new uplift brassiere that makes dresses look better on flappers' slender figures. It's the start of Maiden Form, which will eventually gross tens of millions of dollars a year.

1923 The betting game of "policy," popular in the 1700s, is reborn in Harlem as the numbers game.

1924 George Gershwin gives the first performances of his "Rhapsody in Blue" at Aeolian Hall with the Paul Whiteman Orchestra.

1924 International Business Machines (IBM) is the new name of the 1911 Computing-Tabulating-Recording Company. Its data calculating machines will lead to generations of computers.

1924 Macy's on Herald Square holds its first Thanksgiving Day parade. A new addition to the huge department store adds twelve acres of selling space.

Louis Armstrong by Frances Feist

The Harlem Renaissance movement draws black writers and artists from all over the country. White publishers become interested in black writers such as Claude McKay, Zora Neale Hurston, Countee Cullen, and Langston Hughes: "Hold fast to dreams, for if dreams die, life is a broken-winged bird that cannot fly."

1924 The dramatist Eugene O'Neill and the future international star Paul Robeson join forces on O'Neill's *All God's Chillun Got Wings* at New York's Provincetown Playhouse.

1925 The Brotherhood of Sleeping Car Porters is organized in Harlem by A. Philip Randolph.

Socialites, business moguls, and gangsters are among those who visit Polly Adler's popular house of prostitution off Riverside Drive.

1925 Robert Moses begins his forty-year rule as the City's master builder. He loves cars. His poorly planned construction of highways, bridges, parks, and housing projects blights old neighborhoods and undercuts mass transit, although it provides an enormous number of jobs.

Robert Moses

1925 *The New Yorker* begins publication with funds from the Fleischmann Yeast Company family. Editor Harold Ross hires E. B. White to write essays about nature and his beloved city.

". . . New York, at the beginning of March, is a hoyden we would not care to miss—a drafty wench, her temperature up and down, full of bold promises and dust in the eye."—Writer E. B. White

1925   The Marx Brothers hit the New York stage in *The Cocoanuts* by George S. Kaufman and Irving Berlin. New York City will never be the same again once Groucho, Harpo, Zeppo, and Chico have had a go at it.

The Marx Brothers

1925   One of the world's most beautiful synagogues, the 1868 Moorish-style Emanu-El, seats 2,000. The 42nd Street location has become commercial, so the congregation sells its building and moves uptown to Fifth Avenue and 65th Street.

1925   First baseman Lou Gehrig joins the Yankees for 2,130 consecutive games.

1925   Madison Square Garden has a new location on Eighth Avenue and 50th Street. The Garden is designed for boxing and wrestling, but it also hosts ballet, the circus, ice shows, basketball, and track.

> ❧
>
> **Mohawk Indians from Quebec work on the perilously high steel-beam construction of skyscrapers and bridges that are part of the building boom.**

1926   Radio is a uniting force in the City. NBC is started by powerful RCA, General Electric, and Westinghouse Corporation businessmen.

1926   The advertising industry, big business since World War I, begins its campaign to break the taboo against women smoking.

1926   Acid but funny Dorothy Parker begins to mock humanity in *The New Yorker* as well as at the Algonquin Round Table.

1926   Breakfast cereal magnate Marjorie Post moves into her new Fifth Avenue triplex, which has fifty-four rooms, including a pool, ballroom, bakery, and sun porch. Rent: $75,000 a year.

1927   Cars no longer have to take the ferries between New York and New Jersey. You can cross the state line under the Hudson River by taking the Holland Tunnel.

1927   The Brooklyn Museum opens a grand new Beaux Arts building.

1927   Charles Lindbergh is given the biggest ticker-tape parade ever on his return from the first solo transatlantic flight—New York to Paris—in the *Spirit of St. Louis*.

1927   A New Yorker can talk to a Londoner via transatlantic telephone for $75 for three minutes.

1927   A new invention called television is demonstrated at Bell Telephone's laboratories on West Street.

1927   "You ain't heard nothin' yet, folks," says Al Jolson in the first great musical-talkie, *The Jazz Singer*, a Lower East Side story.

1927   Yeshiva University is founded in Washington Heights. Today it is the oldest and largest Jewish institution for higher education in the country.

1927   Babe Ruth hits sixty home runs for a season record that stands for thirty-four years.

1929   Overcrowded Blackwell's Island Prison (on what is now Roosevelt Island) finds room for Mae West, who is incarcerated for staging her play, *Sex*.

1929   Popeye and his wife, Olive Oyl, are given comic strip life by the New York cartoonist Elzie Crisler Segar, and sales of spinach soar.

1929   New York has 401 reported murders. Chicago has more.

1929   The stock market crashes on Tuesday, October 29, ushering in the Great Depression, which is only ended by World War II jobs and production.

1930s Black jazz musicians give New York a nickname: the Big Apple.

Billie Holiday, "Lady Day," sings in Harlem for eighteen dollars a week. She goes on to win acclaim for her distinctive vocal style and phrasing at Café Society in the Village. Her 1939 song "Strange Fruit," popular and political, is about the lynching of blacks in the south.

1930 The new interdenominational Riverside Church at 120th Street overlooks the Hudson and seats 2,500. The tower houses a five-octave carillon with an hour bell that is the largest carillon bell ever cast. The church will become a center for integration and activism.

The Catholic organizing structure of the City is still the local parish, as it has been since the 1840s. The Church of Our Lady of Lourdes in Bushwick, Brooklyn, has re-created the grotto of Lourdes behind the altar. Parishioners go there to ask for help and leave their crutches hanging up when they walk away.

1930 A shantytown called Hoover Valley, or Forgotten Man's Gulch, springs up in hallowed Central Park. Other "Hoovervilles" appear wherever there is open space in the five boroughs.

Riverside Church

Apple seller

1930 Surplus apples are sold by jobless men and women on City streets; but the 6,000 peddlers unnerve City Hall, and by the spring of 1931, the sales are banned.

1930 Seventeen percent of the City is Italian American.

1930 Edward Hopper paints *Early Sunday Morning*, an empty street of low brick buildings (Seventh Avenue). *Nighthawks* (1942) is another of his portraits of a New York state of mind.

1930 Eleventh Avenue is made safer this year when railroad tracks are moved over to the wharves and a hundred terrifying railroad crossings on "Death Avenue" cease to exist.

1931 The George Washington Bridge is the longest suspension bridge in the world. The lower level, which New Yorkers call Martha after George's wife, is added in 1962.

The Little Red Lighthouse and the Great Gray Bridge by Hildegarde Swift and Lynd Ward (1942) is a favorite book for City kids. The lighthouse still stands today on the Hudson shore.

1931 The fantastical Chrysler Building opens, seventy-seven stories high and the epitome of Art Deco style.

1931 The Empire State Building, dignified and sleek, will be the tallest building in the world for forty years, but businesses are slow to lease office space in it. Despite the Depression, it is completed early and under budget.

1932 John D. Rockefeller, Jr. uses his own money to build Rockefeller Center and gives Depression New York jobs and hope. The finished center and its plaza become one of the great midtown tourist attractions, especially at Christmas when the tree is lit. The tradition dates from 1931 when a tree was put up by the center's construction workers for their own celebration.

Hoover Valley in Central Park

The Chrysler Building

1932   Breadlines.

1932   "Playboy" Mayor Jimmy Walker resigns because of corruption charges.

1932   Joseph Cornell, American realist sculptor, shows his first shadow boxes. He lives a reclusive life in a house on Utopia Parkway in Flushing until his death in 1972.

1932   The vaudeville comedian Jack Benny broadcasts the first of his twenty-three years of radio shows. Eternally thirty-nine and naturally stingy, Benny transfers to television in the 1950s.

1932   The song "Brother, Can you Spare a Dime?" by Yip Harburg and the composer Jay Gorney expresses the national pain and anger at what is happening to the American dream.

The artist Diego Rivera's RCA Building fresco, *Man at the Crossroads*, is demolished in 1934 because Lenin appears in it.

Building the Empire State by Lewis Hine

1932   The 6,000-seat Radio City Music Hall opens as the world's largest indoor theater, with a huge Wurlitzer organ. People come in droves, and the Sixth Avenue el drops patrons off at the door.

1932   Well over a million and a half men, women, and children in the City receive public or private relief. And counting.

Bread Line by *Reginald Marsh*

The Rockettes at Radio City

1933 Prohibition is lifted under the Twenty-first Amendment.

1933 King Kong falls for Fay Wray, escapes from captivity, and has the run of the City in the film classic. The gorilla climbs the new Empire State Building, where he is buzzed by planes and finally killed.

1933 Three great steamship piers are built on the Hudson River between 48th and 52nd Streets in anticipation of huge European liners like the *Normandie* and the *Queen Mary*.

1933 The A and the F trains start service on the IND, which is the first City-run subway, modern and efficient.

1933 Dorothy Day starts the *Catholic Worker* and helps intellectuals and workers join forces for social reform. She has supervised a shelter on the Bowery for ten years.

Women's Temperance Union during Prohibition

Vote for La Guardia! Born in 1892, mother Jewish, father Italian, worked his way through law school by interpreting at Ellis Island (speaks Italian, Yiddish, Hungarian, German, and Serbo-Croatian). Tough young labor lawyer defended 60,000 striking men's clothing workers. First Italian American elected to Congress. Republican, opposed to Democratic Tammany Hall. Fought Prohibition and racism.

1934 Fiorello La Guardia is sworn in as mayor and remains in office for three terms, until 1945. Having been a congressman who worked for New Deal relief programs, he knows how to get money out of Washington. It's a shock for the City to have an honest man in charge.

1934 A 2 percent City sales tax is collected, to be used for relief for the unemployed. Mayor La Guardia has always opposed a sales tax, but has no choice.

1934 The new owners of the 1914 Apollo Theatre on 125th Street allow blacks into the audience. Bessie Smith sings the blues in one of the first shows.

1935 Seven percent of the nation's people on relief live in the City. Its relief agencies are overwhelmed.

1935 President Franklin D. Roosevelt's New Deal sets up the Works Progress Ad-

Bessie Smith

ministration (WPA), which gets more than half the federal budget for the year. It's a lifeline for the City. Most New Yorkers in the WPA work on playgrounds, beaches, road repair, schools, and hospitals. Others teach, run day care, fix teeth. Thousands of actors, painters, writers, and photographers produce extraordinary work for and about the City.

1935 The Depression is destroying Harlem's local economy, and people crowd into apartments divided into tiny units. Despair ignites rioting. Three die.

1935 The new Hayden Planetarium on 81st Street shows 9,000 stars in the southern and northern hemispheres.

1935 The nation's first public housing project opens in rehabilitated tenements on the Lower East Side at Avenue A and 3rd Street. Lucky tenants who get a place in First Houses are finally free of tenement misery, and have hot water and a private toilet, all for $220 a year. About a third of the original tenements have been torn down, so the new tenants have air and light, too. The City Housing Authority is just getting started.

1935 Two years after the end of Prohibition, Alcoholics Anonymous (AA) is founded by Bill Wilson and Dr. Robert H. Smith, who spread the word through church groups.

1935 The East River Drive is begun as a WPA project.

> ❧
>
> "The Mob slipped into the regular life of the city, selling not just vice and booze and gambling but concrete, garbage collection, children's frocks, justice and politics, taxing what was built, trucked or carted away as though it was a second government."—Writer Michael Pye

1935 Big Six gangsters have divvied up the City and control the waterfront, gambling, narcotics, bail bonds, and the extortion racket. Prosecutor Thomas Dewey is appointed to run the likes of Bugsy Siegel and Meyer Lansky out of town. Lucky Luciano is put behind bars for thirty to fifty, but after ten years he is deported to Italy.

The Savoy Ballroom

> ❧
>
> At Harlem's Savoy Ballroom, 5,000 blacks and whites do the Lindy Hop to the music of top jazz bands.

First Houses

1935   A seven-foot alligator is hauled out of a manhole on East 123rd Street by two teenage boys shoving snow down the hole. The Sanitation Department incinerates the reptile, but it lives on in rumors of alligators prowling the New York sewers.

1935   Hospital insurance can be had under the "three cents a day plan."

1936   *Life* magazine is immediately popular for its photo-journalism; it is another coup for Henry Luce of *Time.*

1936   Otto Bettmann manages to leave Hitler's Germany with his collection of 25,000 prints and negatives. He opens the Bettmann Archive in New York.

1936   The Yankees sign up Joe DiMaggio and go on to win the series against the Giants.

1936   The Triborough Bridge links Queens, Manhattan, and the Bronx. Toll: twenty-five cents.

1937   Manhattan along the Hudson River begins its decades-long difficulties with the new elevated West Side Highway, which routes traffic up to 72nd Street from the Battery. The City is more cut off from its river than ever.

1937   The musical *Pins and Needles* is sponsored by the International Ladies Garment Workers' Union and runs for 1,108 performances.

1937   The Lincoln Tunnel opens its first tube under the Hudson River. In the 1990s, forty million vehicles a year make it the world's busiest tunnel.

1937   The City's first federally financed and constructed public housing opens at 151st Street and the Harlem River Drive. Harlem River Houses have plazas and trees, a clinic and a nursery. In Brooklyn the larger Williamsburg Houses contain over 1,600 apartments. The abstract artist Stuart Davis's Federal Art Project murals jazz up the complex.

1938   The City's new charter says goodbye to the Board of Aldermen and hello to proportional representation in the City Council. The non-proportional Board of Estimate is the most powerful governing body (but see 1990). The charter gathers the old housing bureaus together into the Department of Housing. It also limits the City's debt.

1938   The renovated Cloisters opens as a branch of the Metropolitan Museum of Art. The quiet hilltop museum in Fort Tryon Park was pieced together from twelfth- and thirteenth-century French and Spanish monasteries. Its medieval art includes the Unicorn Tapestries. The Museum was expanded with the financial help of John D. Rockefeller, Jr., who gave the City the sixty acres of historic ground as well.

1938   The first "xerograph" copy is made in Astoria, Queens. The trade name Xerox comes from the Greek word *xeros*, meaning dry.

1938   "Wrong way Corrigan" makes depressed New York laugh when he outwits the authorities who refuse him permission to fly his plane to Europe. He takes off from Floyd Bennett Field in Brooklyn, claiming he'll fly solo to Los Angeles, but instead turns east for Dublin. A million fans celebrate his hoax at a ticker-tape parade when he returns.

1938   "The War of the Worlds" puts fear into vulnerable hearts. There is a stampede out of town after this radio play is broadcast on Orson Welles's Mercury Theater of the Air. Welles and radio producer Bill Spier walk out of the studio into a panicked city.

1938   Mayor La Guardia persuades New York State to adopt a constitutional amendment that will help the economy in the long run. Article 17, Section 1, approved by legislators and voters, asserts that "the aid, care and support of the needy are public concerns and shall be provided by the State." The U.S. Constitution and most states have no such article.

1938   The heavyweight champion of the world, Joe Louis, demolishes Max Schmeling in a rematch in Yankee Stadium.

1939   A Nazi "Americanism" rally at Madison Square Garden on February 22, organized by the German-American Bund, denounces the Jews' hatred of Nazis in front of a huge poster of George Washington and draws 22,000.

1939   A month later half a million spectators watch an anti-Nazi "stop Hitler" march. On the podium Mayor La Guardia condemns the Nazi invasion of Czechoslovakia.

1939   Batman fights crime in Gotham City (New York) in his first appearance in *Detective Comics.*

1939 SEE TOMORROW TODAY! The World's Fair in Queens welcomes 45 million visitors. A little guide to the City's history is published for the occasion by the renowned City scholar I. N. Phelps Stokes. The guide is a condensed version of his six-volume *Iconography of Manhattan Island* (1915–1928), which is illustrated with historic documents, maps, and prints.

1939 New York Municipal Airport opens. It has been built with $45 million from the WPA. It is renamed La Guardia Airport in 1947.

1939 The Bronx-Whitestone Bridge opens in time to take Bronx people to the World's Fair as well as to the new airport.

Left and below: The Cloisters

1939 The Museum of Modern Art (MOMA) moves into its new building on West 53rd Street. Its Sculpture Garden, one of the peaceful spots in midtown Manhattan, is added in 1953.

1939 City Hall Park is restored. This triangular plot of land between Broadway and Park Row has been kept a public space since it was the Commons, the settlement's grazing grounds, under the Dutch in the 1600s.

1939 The Yankees win the World Series despite their farewell to Lou Gehrig, who leaves the team because he has *amyotropic lateral sclerosis*, "Lou Gehrig's disease."

1940s In the great mass migration of the 1930s and 1940s, 340,000 blacks flee the poverty and racism of the South and come to New York. Two hundred thousand blacks live in Harlem alone. Frustration and despair fuel a riot in 1943.

1940s Mamie Phipps Clark and Kenneth Clark, both Columbia PhDs, research children's self-image, using white and black dolls. Their findings will play an important role in the breakthrough 1954 U.S. Supreme Court decision, Brown v. Board of Educa-

Seventh Avenue Subway by James Kerr

tion. The Clarks will fight to end pervasive segregation in New York City schools.

1940 The new Midtown Tunnel carries a growing volume of traffic between Queens and Manhattan. The Brooklyn-Battery Tunnel will do the same between Brooklyn and Manhattan, but work is suspended during World War II, and the tunnel is not completed until 1950.

1940 The City buys up the IRT and BMT subway lines from private operators and runs them so well, along with the IND line, that the first year's profit is $28 million.

1940 Tiffany & Company moves to its famous 57th Street and Fifth Avenue corner store.

Mayor Fiorello La Guardia

1940 The first New York City blood bank is opened by a surgeon who is not allowed to donate his own blood because he is black.

1940 *Native Son* is written under a Guggenheim grant by Richard Wright, author of the 1937 *Guide to Harlem*, which he compiled as part of the Federal Writers Project.

1940 The Metropolitan Opera comes free to Saturday afternoon radio audiences.

1940 A bridge over Newtown Creek between Brooklyn and Queens is named the Kosciuszko Bridge after the Polish hero of the American Revolution.

1941 Duke Ellington and Billy Strayhorn "Take the A Train."

1941 "Never underestimate the power of a woman," cautions a *Ladies' Home Journal* advertising campaign.

1941 Two elderly sisters, Mayflower descendants, charitably murder a dozen old men and bury them in the basement of their Brooklyn house. Joseph Kesselring's *Arsenic and Old Lace* is a great wartime hit on Broadway.

1941 Adam Clayton Powell, Jr. is the first black member of the City Council and later the first black representative to Congress from the northeast, representing Harlem from 1944 through the late 1960s.

1942 Parkchester in the Bronx is not a city but a vast housing development, one of the first of its kind in the country, with 12,273 apartments in buildings on a 129-acre site. It was built by Met Life, which checks tenants carefully before admitting them, but until the 1960s only whites need apply.

1942 *The New York Herald Tribune* is the only paper in the nation to publish an accurate front-page story on a report that the Nazis have systematically murdered 700,000 Jews in Poland and Lithuania, 125,000 in Rumania, and 200,000 in White Russia and the Ukraine.

1942 Bomb rubble from England, brought in as ballast on British ships, is used for fill under the East River (FDR) Drive. The rubble is the result of German bombing raids.

1942 Frank Sinatra sings at the New York Paramount Theater to crowds of swooning teenagers.

1942 The City Council bans pinball machines. Mayor La Guardia goes after the machines with a sledgehammer, saying that kids steal nickels from their mothers to play, and the money goes to organized crime.

1943 *Oklahoma* by Rodgers and Hammerstein opens on Broadway and runs for 2,212 performances. In this groundbreaking musical, songs set mood, develop character, and carry the plot forward.

1943 *A Tree Grows in Brooklyn* is Betty Smith's best-selling novel about a young girl growing up in a Williamsburg tenement.

1943 Rent control begins as a federal law that expires in 1950, though New York and other states keep renewing it. The controls restrict increases landlords can impose and allow families to stay put and build neighborhoods.

1944 *On the Town*, a musical by Leonard Bernstein, Betty Comden, and Adolph Green, brings three sailors on leave to New York City, where they get their girls.

1945 An air force light bomber crashes into the Empire State Building on a Saturday and kills three in the air and ten on the ground.

1945 New York learns that two Japanese cities are leveled and hundreds of thousands of people killed or maimed when American atomic bombs are dropped on Hiroshima and Nagasaki. JAPAN SURRENDERS, END OF WAR! screams *The New York Times* headline.

1945 In an international gesture, New York renames Sixth Avenue the Avenue of the Americas, but most New Yorkers never accept the name.

1945 E. B. White's *Stuart Little* is about a mouse born to an average American family living in a pleasant home near Central Park. "Not every doctor can look into a mouse's ear without laughing."

1946 The New York pediatrican Dr. Benjamin Spock's *Common Sense Book of Baby and Child Care* introduces feeding-on-demand to generations of parents.

1947 The Dodgers hire Jackie Robinson, the first African American to break the twentieth-century color bar in the major leagues. It takes heroic restraint to fight bigotry and win election to the Baseball Hall of Fame.

New York School post-war artists like Willem De Kooning, Robert Motherwell, Franz Kline, Mark Rothko, and Arshile Gorky drop representational art for form, line, and color. Jackson Pollock goes for "action painting."

1947 The first Tony Awards, named after actress Antoinette "Tony" Perry, are presented for excellence on the Broadway stage.

1947 In one month 6.3 million New Yorkers are vaccinated against smallpox. The City's drive to stop a threatened epidemic succeeds at unprecedented levels because vaccination is voluntary, and New Yorkers still have a war-effort mindset, notes historian Judith Leavitt.

1947 In the New York chapter of a modern-day inquisition, Hollywood studio executives at the Waldorf-Astoria Hotel draw up a blacklist of 300 writers, directors, and actors suspected of Communist leanings.

> As the Cold War continues, public school children are issued dog tags and their teachers are required to take a loyalty oath.

1947 The Collyer brothers, two of New York's eccentrics, have lived with piles of garbage, rats, engine parts, fourteen grand pianos, and old newspapers in a house on Fifth Avenue at 128th Street. Police find them both dead after a mysterious telephone tip.

1947 A snowstorm the day after Christmas tops the blizzard of 1888, with 26.4 inches of snow. Traffic stops for three days. Young children can play in the street. It's quiet.

1948 It's the golden anniversary of Greater New York, and the City has more than doubled its population in the fifty years since consolidation.

1948 "There are 8 million stories in the naked city; this has been one of them." *The Naked City*, the classic film noir starring New York, morphs into a favorite television series in the 1950s.

1948 The transit fare jumps from a nickel to a dime after forty-four years.

1948 Idlewild, the City's new international airport in Queens, will become the largest commercial airport in the world. It is renamed after John F. Kennedy in 1963.

1948 City garbage, until now dumped into the Atlantic, goes to Fresh Kills, Staten Island, which has been chosen as the City's landfill site. By the 1990s the garbage is piled high on 2,100 acres, and Staten Island's outrage piles up, too. (See 1998)

1949 Kate Wollman gives $600,000 to the City for a grand ice-skating rink in Central Park. Brooklyn's Prospect Park opens its own Wollman Rink in 1962.

1949 The alto saxophonist Charlie Parker, known as Bird, performs at his new club, Birdland, on Broadway.

1950s "New York is an ugly city, a dirty city. Its climate is a scandal, its politics are used to frighten children, its traffic is madness, its competition is murderous. But there is one thing about it—once you have lived in New York and it has become your home, no place else is good enough."
—Writer John Steinbeck

1950s Until the mid-fifties, New York City is the center of television production, with CBS, NBC, ABC, and Du Mont amassing great profits and giving America Jackie Gleason and Sid Caesar in exchange.

> "The entertainment industry was an inviting target for McCarthyism. Blacklists were enforced by radio and television networks, their commercial sponsors, and advertising agencies, who feared retaliation from the political right if they did not comply."—Historian Ellen W. Schrecker

1950 The census counts a city of 7,891,957 people and reports that 56 percent of the population is foreign-born or of foreign or mixed parentage.

1950 Metropolitan New York, including the surrounding suburbs, is the largest metropolis in the world, with a population of 12.3 million.

1950 The Port Authority Bus Terminal opens; it is the biggest in the world.

1950 City College's basketball team wins both the NCAA and NIT basketball tournaments, the only time in history one team wins both. Next year college basketball in the City is in shambles when players from seven colleges are indicted for shaving points for gambling.

1950 The United Nations Secretariat Building opens on a seventeen-acre tract along the East River. John D. Rockefeller, Jr. donated $8.5 million to buy the strip of land from real estate mogul William Zeckendorf.

1950 Alternate-side-of-the-street parking begins. It allows for street cleaning and creates the ritual of moving the car. Fifty years later New Yorkers drink coffee and read the paper sitting in their parked cars waiting for their spaces to become legal.

United Nations

> ❧
>
> In a battle with the automobile, from 1951 to 1966, First and Second Avenues, Third and Lexington, Broadway, Sixth, Seventh and Eighth, and finally Fifth and Madison Avenues, are made one-way streets to speed up Manhattan's traffic.

1951 At the U.S. Courthouse on Foley Square, Julius and Ethel Rosenberg and Morton Sobell are found guilty of selling atomic secrets to the Soviets. The Rosenbergs are executed in 1953.

1951 The Dodgers lose the pennant in the bottom of the ninth. Fans go suicidal when Bobby Thomson of the Giants hits a game-winning home run off Ralph Branca.

1951 *The Catcher in the Rye* by New Yorker J. D. Salinger, published this year, becomes a bible for teenagers.

1950 Vincent Impellitteri becomes mayor and appoints the power broker Robert Moses to head the Slum Clearance Committee.

1952 Dr. Virginia Apgar at Columbia Presbyterian Hospital develops the Apgar Score for assessing the health of newborn infants.

1952 Lever House brings the first wall of soaring glass to Park Avenue's unbroken stone façade and the first glass office building to a mostly residential avenue.

1952 During a drought the City seeds clouds over the reservoirs, hoping to create rain.

1952 "The Today Show" stars Dave Garroway and J. Fred Muggs, the chimpanzee, which gets the kids to watch, too.

1952 Dave Brubeck brings his progressive jazz to the City.

1953 Robert Wagner begins twelve years as mayor.

Mayor Robert F. Wagner

1953 The New York City Transit Authority is established to run the City's subways and buses. The fare goes to fifteen cents, and subway tokens are introduced.

Lever House

1953 Acute poverty in Puerto Rico has been sending people here since the war. In this peak year, 58,500 Puerto Ricans arrive, looking for jobs in the postwar economy. It's the first mass migration to come by plane.

Many Puerto Ricans come to El Barrio (East 100s), where they find some of the comforts of home, such as food and language. In 1969 El Museo del Barrio opens as a cultural center.

1954   Half a million commuters come into Manhattan daily.

1954   In Elia Kazan's film *On the Waterfront*, starring Marlon Brando and Eva Marie Saint, Brooklyn longshoremen confront "the butchers in camel hair coats." The following year, *A View from the Bridge*, a play by Arthur Miller, takes a look at another slice of life in Red Hook, Brooklyn.

1954   Bill Haley and the Comets record "Rock Around the Clock" at Decca Records on West 70th Street.

1955   Mayor Wagner submits a record budget: $1,783,086,557.

1955   New York University biochemist Severo Ochoa announces "the synthesis of ribonucleic acid (RNA), a basic constituent of all living tissues. It is a giant step toward the creation of life in the laboratory out of inert materials."—Historian James Trager

1955   Walk/Don't Walk signs begin to flash at intersections.

1955   The contralto Marian Anderson is the first black singer to perform at the Metropolitan Opera. She is well known for singing both opera and spirituals.

1955   *Eloise* by Kay Thompson introduces the naughty child who lives at the Plaza.

1955   The first issue of *The Village Voice* is printed.

1956   Twenty volunteers help public school teachers under the School Volunteer Program, the first of its kind in the nation. In 1998, 9,000 trained tutors in the City help 140,000 children.

Marian Anderson

Yankees, 1954

1957 Elvis is seen only from the waist up on "The Ed Sullivan Show."

1957 *West Side Story*, a Romeo and Juliet tale about two rival gangs in Hell's Kitchen, opens on Broadway. The score is by Leonard Bernstein, with lyrics by Stephen Sondheim. Arthur Laurents writes the book and Jerome Robbins is director and choreographer.

1957 The last trolleys are seen on New York City streets when the Queensboro Bridge line goes out of service.

1957 In their final game at Ebbets Field the Brooklyn Dodgers—"Dem Bums"—beat Pittsburgh 2–0. In 1958 both the Dodgers and the New York Giants move to California.

1957 Althea Gibson, the first black world champion tennis player, is honored with a ticker-tape parade. She learned to play on the 155th Street public courts.

1958 Alvin Ailey creates his American Dance Theater to give black dancers a place in the world of dance.

1958 The bronze and glass Seagram Building, designed by Mies van der Rohe, is set back from Park Avenue on a plaza. "The brilliant success of Seagram led the city in its 1961 revision of the zoning code to encourage other tall towers on plazas," notes architecture critic Paul Goldberger. Unfortunately, many of the plaza's first imitations are skimpy and dreary.

1959 Brooke Astor's husband Vincent dies and she begins her philanthropic career, a labor of love that over the next 38 years will give $200 million to City institutions ranging from the New York Public Library to a small family literacy program in lower Manhattan. She inspires fellow philanthropists.

1959 The Solomon R. Guggenheim Museum, designed by Frank Lloyd Wright, opens on Fifth Avenue. Wright dies this year.

1959 Ground is broken on Manhattan's West Side for Lincoln Center for the Performing Arts. Thousands of residents in the neighborhood are pushed out to find other housing. In 1961 the movie of *West Side Story* is filmed in the emptied-out neighborhood.

1959 Hell's Kitchen in the West 40s, a hotbed of gangs and poverty for much of its history, is given a milder name: Clinton.

The Guggenheim Museum

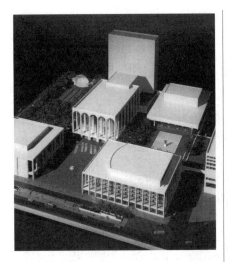

Model of Lincoln Center

1959 *Brown Girl, Brownstones* is Paule Marshall's finely wrought novel of Barbadian immigrants in Brooklyn during the 1930s and 1940s.

1960 For fifty years New York Harbor, the cornerstone of the City's commerce and glory, has been the busiest port in the world. But the Port Authority of New York and New Jersey routes the new container ships to Elizabeth, New Jersey, and the New York waterfront begins its decline (but see 1998).

1960 The violinist Isaac Stern leads the fight to save Carnegie Hall from demolition.

1960 *The Fantasticks*, the musical by Harvey Schmidt and Tom Jones, opens and is still running today after more than 16,000 performances.

1960 This year, more than two-thirds of the nation's better-known artists are living and working in their mecca, New York City.

New York Harbor at 2 p.m., January 16, 1961

1961 City University of New York is formed from four senior and four community colleges. Today CUNY's medical school, law school, graduate school, and seventeen colleges serve a total of 200,000 students.

1961 A new state law allows New York City police to live outside the City.

1961 A new zoning resolution makes small-scale, step-by-step real estate development a thing of the past. Lefrak City, a privately owned apartment superproject for 5,000 families, opens in 1962–1967.

1962 City College Professor Kenneth B. Clark founds HARYOU (Harlem Youth Opportunities Unlimited), which in 1964 will become part of the federal government's War on Poverty.

1962 Free performances of Shakespeare's plays, which Joseph Papp has been producing from a flatbed truck for eight years, have a permanent new home in Central Park, the open-air Delacorte Theater.

1962 The New York Mets, a new team in the National Baseball League, arrive on the scene and lift the spirits of New Yorkers, who are still mourning the loss of the Dodgers and the Giants to California. Two years later the Mets' park is Shea Stadium.

1963 *The New York Times* headline, November 23: KENNEDY IS KILLED BY SNIPER AS HE RIDES IN CAR IN DALLAS; JOHNSON SWORN IN ON PLANE.

1963 *The New York Mirror* folds as a result of a 114-day newspaper strike. Eight City dailies drop to three in the next few years as people get their news from talking heads on television.

Shea Stadium

1963 The massive fifty-nine-story Pan Am Building rises above Grand Central Terminal and destroys Park Avenue vistas.

1963 Jean Neditch of Queens founds Weight Watchers with a high-protein diet developed by Norman Jolliffe of the New York City Department of Health.

1964 The Verrazano Narrows Bridge connects Brooklyn and Staten Island. Today the forty-two-mile, five-borough annual American Youth Hostel bike trip ends with crossing the bridge to Staten Island.

1964 J. Raymond Jones, political strategist, becomes the first black leader of Tammany Hall. In the 1920s he founded the City's key

black political organization, and since then "the Harlem Fox" has been working for his constituency as district leader and City Councilman.

1964 The New York World's Fair opens in Flushing Meadows and attracts 51 million visitors during April to October of 1964 and 1965. Sangria is introduced at the Spanish Pavilion.

Lew Alcindor, soon known as Kareem Abdul-Jabbar, plays basketball at Power Memorial High School. He will become the all-time leading scorer in the National Basketball Association. Julius Erving—"Dr. J"—will become one of the NBA's greatest players.

In eight years, 1955 to 1963, New York City doctors win five Nobel Prizes for their medical discoveries.

1964 Mayor Wagner asks Martin Luther King, Jr. for his advice after a three-night riot in Harlem kills one and seriously wounds 141. The riot results from the killing of a young man by a white police lieutenant. Racial demonstrations in the City are part of civil rights bitterness nationwide. New York City is a center for civil rights activism in this decade.

1964 The Beatles arrive from England and charm New York audiences.

World's Fair in Queens

Verrazano Narrows Bridge under construction

1964 Kitty Genovese is murdered on a street in Queens while neighbors fail to act.

1965 Malcolm X (El-Hajj Malik El-Shabazz) is assassinated at the Audubon Ballroom on 165th Street as he speaks for peaceful coexistence.

1965 New York City has close to a million industrial workers and almost half a million people on welfare. Automation looms over the workforce.

1965 Helen Gurley Brown, the author of *Sex and the Single Girl*, is brought in to save a fiction magazine, *Cosmopolitan*. The sexual revolution picks up steam.

1965 Helena Rubinstein dies at age ninety-four. She has worn a white doctor's coat to give her ads scientific flair. Her business is worth $60 million.

1965 "Save water: shower with a friend." The City has been suffering a drought for five years, and this is its driest year.

1965 On a night in November, pilots flying over the City are astonished to see it disappear. Due to the blackout of the northeastern U.S., New York handles a record 62 million phone calls in one day. Station WINS, covering the blackout, announces the era of all-news radio.

1965 Preservationists howl as monumental Pennsylvania Station, with its Tuscan columns and acres of vaulted glass domes, is demolished over a three-year period, 1963–1966. The City's Landmarks Preservation Commission is the phoenix that rises from the ashes.

1965 After forty-one years the door swings open again. The Hart-Celler Act dramatically alters immigration to the United States—and especially to the City. People flood in from the Caribbean and Africa, then from Asia, Central America, and Eastern Europe, making New York City a map of the world.

Dominicans fleeing their troubled country are the largest immigrant group settling in New York City. Washington Heights and Jackson Heights become Dominican neighborhoods.

Pennsylvania Station

1965 Chants of "Hare Krishna" drone in New York streets. Berobed youth, followers of Hindu Swami Prabhupada, chant and beg for a living.

1966 The day John V. Lindsay becomes mayor, TWU leader Mike Quill leads a twelve-day strike of 33,000 transit workers, shutting down the largest transit system in the world. Lost wages amount to as much as $25 million a day because people can't get to work. The subway fare rises to twenty cents.

1966 A twenty-five-day newspaper blackout is followed by a thirty-three-day dock strike.

1966 The old Metropolitan Opera moves from its glorious Broadway and 39th Street house to its new home in Lincoln Center. The architecture critic Nathan Silver calls the Met's demolition of the old house "the archetype of unjustified destruction."

The cast of Hair

❧

Transatlantic passengers now take planes instead of ocean liners, and the West Side piers are abandoned. Docks begin to crumble into the river, and a spooky silence replaces the bustle of profitable wharves.

1966 Parks Commissioner Thomas Hoving closes Central Park to cars on summer Sundays, opening the roads to walkers and cyclists.

1967 Phoenix House, one of very few treatment programs for a growing drug epidemic, opens on West 85th Street.

1967 The Public Broadcasting Act is signed into law, and the New York area gets its invaluable Channel Thirteen.

1967 Martin Luther King, Jr. leads 125,000 anti-Vietnam War protesters from Central Park to the United Nations. Later, another group of demonstrators blocks the Whitehall Induction Center and is arrested.

❧

Haitians in greatly increasing numbers flee the Duvalier regime and move to the City. Many hope to return to their country with its rich culture. By the late 1990s, 300,000 Haitians live and work in New York City.

1967 *Hair*, the hippie musical, is the inaugural production at the Public Theater, and speaks for long-haired, tie-dyed, love-beaded youth.

1967 Piri Thomas comes of age in Spanish Harlem. His book, *Down These Mean Streets*, has a glossary listing bodega, dinero, nada, mañana, loco, caramba, cuchifritos, corazon, and other words that have become part of City talk.

1967 During the "long hot summer," riots threaten the nation. A shirt-sleeved Mayor Lindsay walks Spanish Harlem streets after a Puerto Rican youth is killed, and New York courageously spares itself the fate of other burned-out American cities.

1967 Garbage piles up on sidewalks and starts to stink while 10,000 sanitation workers strike for nine days.

1968 *The New York Times* headlines. April 5: MARTIN LUTHER KING IS SLAIN IN MEMPHIS. June 6: KENNEDY IS DEAD, VICTIM OF ASSASSIN.

1968 Militant Columbia University students protest the building of a gym in Morningside Park. The plan is cancelled in 1969. They also object to Columbia's real estate policy, which shuts working-class people out of local housing.

> ❦
>
> "Deinstitutionalization." New York State mental institutions start releasing thousands of patients onto the streets. They're supposed to go into supportive community houses where they're reminded to take their medication, but the plan isn't funded and the safety net doesn't work.

1968 New York is the first city in the U.S. to use the emergency 911 telephone line.

1968 Public education comes to a halt in the city for two months when Brooklyn's Ocean Hill–Brownsville district, trying local control, fires nineteen staff members and the United Federation of Teachers goes on the most bitter strike in its history. More than half of the City's public school children are black and Hispanic in a mostly segregated system. The City tries decentralizing the system by creating 32 school districts.

1968 Brooklyn's Shirley Chisholm is elected to Congress and is the first black woman in the U.S. House of Representatives.

1968 *New York* magazine, edited by Clay Felker, starts to recount City life, investigate corruption, and set the style for magazines to come.

1968 Forest Hills' famous tennis tournament is now "open" to professionals as well as amateurs.

1969 Queens residents are incensed at the City's delay in clearing their streets of 20.2 inches of snow. The storm is labeled Mayor Lindsay's Storm.

1969 Barnard women want co-ed dorms and stage a sleep-in.

1969 In Harlem, Mother Hale cares for a drug addict's infant. By 1991 Hale and her physician daughter have nursed over 800 infants through drug withdrawal in Hale House on West 122nd Street.

1969 The SS *Manhattan* batters her way through the frozen Northwest Passage across the top of North America, the first commercial ship to sail the route dreamed of by Henry Hudson and other early explorers.

1969 MEN WALK ON THE MOON, announces *The New York Times* on July 21.

1969 The Stonewall Inn riot starts the gay rights movement as gays protest a raid by police on a Greenwich Village club.

1969 "Sesame Street," produced by Children's Television Workshop in New York, is set in a fictional City neighborhood. Children all over the country learn about kindness and cooperation from the program, which features Jim Henson puppets Big Bird, Oscar the Grouch, and Bert and Ernie.

1969 The underdog Jets win the Superbowl. The Mets amaze their fans and win their first World Series. The Knicks begin their first NBA championship season.

1970 An explosion in a West 11th Street town house kills three members of the antiwar group, the Weathermen.

1970 To make up for inadequate, overcrowded high schools, the City University of New York (CUNY) adopts a policy of open admissions, which guarantees a place for every New York City high school graduate, regardless of grades.

1970 The Penn Central Railroad goes bankrupt. Passenger railroads can't compete with government-funded highways and airports.

1970 *Time and Again* by Jack Finney, a time-travel romance set largely in late-nineteenth-century New York, makes readers fall in love with their City.

1970 In the first New York City Marathon 126 runners race around Central Park four times. In the coming years, the number of runners will grow to 32,000, and the route will thread through all five boroughs.

1970 Herman Badillo, the first Puerto Rican to represent a United States Congressional district in the House of Representatives, has worked his way through law school and Democratic ranks. His political base is the Bronx, where he was borough president. More than 10 percent of the City's population is Puerto Rican: 818,000.

1970 Spaceship Earth is honored on Earth Day, April 21, with a huge demonstration in Central Park against pollution.

1970 As nearly two million people move out of the City during this decade, 800,000 immigrants flock in. They begin to revive old neighborhoods like Brighton Beach and Chinatown, a pattern that will become increasingly clear in the next two decades.

One large immigrant group is from South Korea. Most Koreans arrive with college degrees and intact two- and three-generation families. The *kye*, or credit club, helps them start a profusion of small businesses—10,000 by 1991, including the 24-hour produce and flower markets which colorfully dot City neighborhoods.

1970 The City begins connecting the Brooklyn and Queens water tunnels 600 feet underground. This is a first step in the most expensive capital project in the City's history. Tunnel No. 3, slated for completion in 2020, will bring in a billion gallons of water a day. (See 1998)

McSorley's Old Ale House

1970 From now on, McSorley's Old Ale House, a wonderfully scruffy, exclusively male bar on East 7th Street since 1854, must admit women.

1970 Graffiti infuriates commuters. As the budget for the subways goes down, graffiti painters like Taki 183, a Greek-American teenager, cover cars and walls with their sprawling tags. Eventually, barbed-wire fences enclose subway yards, and minors are prohibited from buying spray paint.

Graffiti at the 91st Street ghost station

1971 The *New York Times* is the first to publish installments from the Pentagon Papers, the government's secret study of the Vietnam War. The government halts publication, but the Supreme Court says to keep printing.

1971 New York City tries Off-Track Betting (OTB) to undercut gambling profits raked in by organized crime, but the underworld flourishes anyway.

1971 Louis Armstrong, known as Satchmo, dies at his house in Corona, Queens, where he has lived for decades. Queens College will open the landmark house as a museum in 2001.

The tram

Louis Armstrong—"Satchmo"

1971 Corona is the setting for the sitcom "All in the Family," which introduces television-watchers to bigot Archie Bunker.

1971 Artists who moved illegally into warehouses south of Houston Street (SoHo) win a zoning victory that allows them to remain in the old cast-iron industrial and commercial buildings. Landmark status for a twenty-six-block area follows in 1973. Rents will soar in the 1980s.

1971 New York sells itself to tourists and for its logo uses the Big Apple, the name black musicians gave the City in the 1930s.

1972 Feminist *Ms.* magazine is launched in New York with Gloria Steinem as editor. It refuses to pander to its advertisers.

1973 Roosevelt Island is a planned residential neighborhood connected to Manhattan by bright red overhead tram cars, and in 1989, the subway. Infamous prisons and asylums once huddled where apartment buildings now stand.

1973 Sweat-equity allows poor people to restore and then own run-down City housing. The Urban Homesteaders begin reclaiming 20,000 apartments.

1973 The movie *Serpico* recounts a real cop's late-1960s battle against systemwide NYPD corruption. Frank Serpico's exceptional courage gave us the Knapp Commission and broke the hold of corrupt authorities.

1973 The Green Guerillas bring community gardens to the City.

1975 The City can't sell its municipal bonds and faces bankruptcy. Inflation brought on by the Vietnam War has made the City's financial situation worse, and many small businesses fail.

1975 A *Daily News* headline announces President Gerald Ford's message to New York: DROP DEAD. But the feds loan nearly $2 billion anyway.

1975 The state forms the Municipal Assistance Corporation to refinance the City's debt, the only way to save the City. Felix Rohatyn heads MAC. Mayor Beame loses all power to MAC and the Emergency Financial Control Board, which make all the financial decisions. Unions lend the City their pension funds.

1975 NBC's "Saturday Night Live" keeps New Yorkers up late and laughing.

1975 A *Chorus Line* moves to Broadway for more than 6,000 performances. Its revenues fund other Public Theater productions for years.

1975 Thirteen thousand fires break out in a twelve-square-mile area of the South Bronx, making it a national symbol of urban devastation.

1976 The City charges tuition at CUNY for the first time since it was founded in 1847. The first six years of open admissions have increased enrollment by 94,000 students to a total of 268,000. Tuition brings enrollment back down; the very poor are shut out.

1976 Over three years the City cuts 65,000 municipal jobs, freezes wages for all other City workers, severely cuts services, and raises subway and bus fares.

1976 The nation's bicentennial is celebrated in New York with Operation Sail, a glorious procession up the Hudson River with tall ships from all over the world. Huge jets of water from fireships salute them. New York is jammed with visitors, and the City rediscovers its waterfront and feels a great lift in its spirits.

1976 Daniel Patrick Moynihan, an alumnus of Hell's Kitchen and former Harvard professor, is elected to the United States Senate. In 1999 he is in his fourth, and last, term representing New York State.

1976 The City's last remaining afternoon paper, *The New York Post*, is bought by the Australian newspaper mogul Rupert Murdoch, who goes all out for sensationalism to grab a new mass readership.

1976 The cartoonist Saul Steinberg does a cover for *The New Yorker* from a Manhattan-centric point of view. The West Side is drawn in wonderful detail, New Jersey is a thin brown strip, and China, Japan, and Russia are bumps on the horizon.

1976 At the World Trade Center, built by the Port Authority, the 110-story Twin Towers and a five-acre Plaza are completed. In 1977 a rock climber inches up one of the towers in four hours, using climbing equipment. The towers have also been used for a daring high-wire act. (But see page 138.)

1976 Farmers bring their apples, collard greens, pumpkins, tomatoes, corn, and chrysanthemums to the gritty yard under the 59th Street Bridge for the first of the City's weekly farmers' markets. Today the Greenmarket thrives in City schoolyards and neighborhood squares, and grosses $15 million a year.

1977 *Saturday Night Fever*, a film based on a *New York* magazine article, is about a Brooklyn teenager with a dreary day job who spends his nights as king of his local disco. Music is by the Bee Gees.

1977 "Son of Sam" David Berkowitz is caught after a yearlong rampage during which he murders five women and a man, maims seven others, and terrifies the City. He claims to be following the orders of a neighbor's dog.

Farmers' market at Broadway and 72nd Street

1977 A heatwave causes a twenty-five-hour blackout. Stores are looted.

1977 In Brooklyn a medical researcher, Raymond V. Damadian, tests the first Magnetic Resonance Imaging scanner.

1977 Citicorp Center breaks a construction slump and brings excitement to mid-Manhattan. The skyscraper's slanted roof changes the skyline. St. Peter's Church on the corner is famous for its jazz vesper services.

1977 President Jimmy Carter comes to the South Bronx and vows to work on urban renewal. The federal program is slow-moving, and Carter later gets involved with his own foundation, Habitat for Humanity. The South Bronx includes a diverse group of neighborhoods that start to come back to life in the 1980s.

1978 The federal government guarantees $1.65 billion worth of loans to the City. New York starts its long recovery. Ed Koch, the new Democratic mayor, helps the City get back on its feet financially.

1978 New York's dog walkers now have to clean up after their pets under the Pooper Scooper Law. Nevertheless, by 1998 the number of dogs in the City doubles to an estimated one million.

World Trade Center's Twin Towers under construction

1978 A three-month strike by ten unions halts publication of newspapers and some magazines.

1978 Women sports reporters gain the right to enter Yankee Stadium locker rooms.

1979 A decade after the state shut down its mental institutions, homelessness is increasing. Robert Hayes, a lawyer and the conscience of the City, sues Governor Carey on behalf of the needy. Severe mental illness, not acoholism, is now the chief cause of homelessness. The state orders the City to provide shelter, but the huge armories lined with beds are frightening and dangerous.

1979 A self-appointed crime-fighting group to be known as the Guardian Angels begins patrolling subways and City streets in red berets.

Above: Citicorp Center
Left: St. Peter's, the Jazz Church, at Citicorp

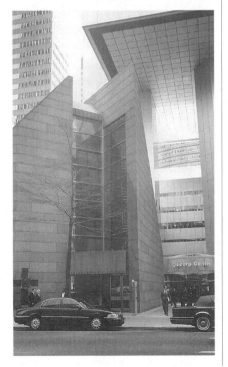

Guardian Angels

1979   Discotheque Studio 54's high-powered owners are sentenced to three and a half years in prison for tax evasion.

1980s   Forest Hills sees a new flood of immigrants from Iran, China, India, the Soviet Union, Israel, Colombia, Romania, Pakistan, and Poland.

1980   The Schomburg Center for Research in Black Culture brings a new $3.8 million study center to 135th Street in Harlem. The center is a research branch of the New York Public Library.

1980   About a quarter of all New Yorkers are black, and a fifth Latino.

1980   Transit workers call a strike that lasts eleven days. People walk to work, and women wear sneakers and socks and carry their good shoes. Comfort wins over style, and sneakers are still in today.

1980   Donald Trump, real estate developer from Queens, guts the Commodore Hotel on 42nd Street to create the Grand Hyatt. It's a splashy beginning to a career that includes the Wollman Rink renovation, Trump Tower on Fifth Avenue, bankruptcy in Atlantic City, and a comeback with a vengeance: Riverside South.

1980   Squatters take over East 13th Street buildings, which the City has held since foreclosures in the late 1970s. The City will finally rout the squatters in 1996.

1980   Manhattan's Columbus Avenue, recently a run-down thoroughfare, begins to smarten up with retail chains and restaurants. Soon it's the chic place for yuppies to go, but small retailers have to move out as their rents are increased.

1980   On December 8 a deranged fan murders Beatle John Lennon in front of the Dakota apartment house on Central Park West. Five years later, in the park across the street, his widow, Yoko Ono, creates a garden called Strawberry Fields after the Beatles song.

1981   Battery Park City is a new breezy riverside neighborhood of stores, housing, and promenades, built partly on twenty-five acres of landfill excavated during the construction of the World Trade Center.

1981   Paul Simon and Art Garfunkel, the folk-rock duo, give a concert on the Great Lawn in Central Park for 500,000 fans, many of whom have come to sing along as well as to listen.

1981   MTV, a cable channel, broadcasts music videos, a new kind of entertainment, twenty-four hours a day from New York, and within twelve years has 210 million subscribers in seventy-one countries.

1981   The identification of the AIDS virus explains the puzzling deaths of dozens of New Yorkers over the past few years from the breakdown of their immune systems.

At Strawberry Fields

1981 GMHC, Gay Men's Health Crisis, is founded by six gay men to provide services to those with AIDS. The organization sponsors the AIDS Walk each May to raise funds.

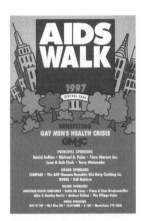

Promenade, Battery Park City

1981   An ambitious new port in Brooklyn opens and just sits there. Container ships have been directed to New Jersey. (See 1998)

1982   800,000 demonstrators gather in Central Park to protest nuclear arms.

1982   Car alarms add to the City's din when New York State reduces insurance rates for cars with alarms, but eventually somebody thinks of outlawing any that wail longer than three minutes.

1982   The City begins to turn the subway system around. The Transit Authority spends about a billion dollars a year for the next thirteen years fixing up the trains and tracks.

1982   The Cathedral Church of St. John the Divine trains local youth in medieval stone-masonry while adding to the carvings in its arched doorways. Its Community Cares program helps 25,000 local people each year.

1983   Many New Yorkers celebrate the centennial of the Brooklyn Bridge by walking across it.

Stone carvings at St. John the Divine

1983   The antisliver law sets height limits for narrow buildings.

1983   "Start spreading the news." The City adopts Kander and Ebb's song "New York, New York" as its official song and uses it to promote the Big Apple.

1984   New York's threatening paranormal entities are set upon by the Ghostbusters.

1984   Bernhard Goetz, subway vigilante, shoots four black youths, paralyzing one, and runs away. Goetz soon turns himself in and is indicted on possession of an illegal weapon. Later he is indicted for attempted murder and acquitted, but in 1996 in the civil trial, he is held liable for a $43 million judgment.

1985   Westway, a $2.3 billion project to build a four-mile long highway, is scrapped, to the delight of many opponents. Marcy Benstock is the hero in this battle for clean air and common sense.

1985   The 1940 Long Island paper *Newsday* expands its territory and starts *New York Newsday.*

1985   Crack cocaine comes in and makes people addicted and crazy. Crime soars. Tiny crack vials with caps of many colors litter the City.

⌘

"Drugs populate the empty landscape, supply the missing heaven, extend the movie into the third dimension. Drugs impose their own structure—customs and language, goals and priorities, rewards and punishments—on lives in which all belief has collapsed."—Writer Luc Sante

1985   Upper West Side and Harlem families begin organizing sports leagues. They overcome urban obstacles that suburban parents can't imagine, like byzantine bureaucracy, homeless encampments in the park, and sky-high fees for gyms. Soon thousands of children are playing baseball, soccer, basketball, and hockey with parent coaches.

⌘

"A walk across the Brooklyn Bridge is not like any other experience in New York, or in any other city. You are at once immersed in the life of the city, and above it: the view of the skyline is stunning; of the river, exciting; and of the bridge itself, pleasingly intimate." —Architecture critic Paul Goldberger

1985 The land under Rockefeller Center is sold by Columbia University for $400 million.

1985 *Crains New York Business* begins publication.

1986 Three black men passing through Howard Beach, Queens, are hounded and brutally assaulted, one killed by a car as he flees. Minister Al Sharpton leads protests after the incident. White initiators of the attack are eventually convicted of manslaughter.

1986 The Parking Violations Bureau is embroiled in a kickback scandal. The Queens Democratic politician Donald Manes, who has taken bribes for eight years, kills himself.

1986 The Jacob K. Javits Convention Center, oceans of mirrored glass, opens on the Hudson River between 34th and 38th Streets. In Congress, Javits worked for health and social welfare and for civil rights.

1986 The centennial of the Statue of Liberty is celebrated after repairs spruce up the largest lady in the world. Tall ships, fireworks, and lots of tourists add to the occasion. Blacks tactfully remind the City that their route to New York was different.

1987 Six-year-old Lisa Steinberg, daughter of a cocaine-addicted professional couple, is starved and beaten to death.

1987 We Can, recyclers on 43rd Street off Tenth Avenue, begins buying discarded soda cans, $25 million worth over the next ten years.

1987 The New York Stock Exchange falls 508 points on Black Monday. The Opulent Eighties are over.

1988 The new zoo in Central Park is small but wonderful, with its climate-controlled rain forest and Antarctic exhibits. Young and old love to watch the seals being fed. Refurbished zoos soon open in Flushing Meadows–Corona Park and Prospect Park.

Jayhawks, Safe Haven Basketball League

Jacob K. Javits Convention Center

Lower East Side Tenement Museum

1988 The City prohibits smoking in public places.

1988 The Lower East Side Tenement Museum is established at 97 Orchard Street. The founders, Ruth J. Abram and Anita Jacobson, aim to illustrate the living conditions many people had to endure around the turn of the century. Schoolchildren and adults go there to learn what it was like.

1988 When the Williamsburg Bridge is judged unsafe for traffic, the City begins to correct long years of deferred maintenance.

1989 Hunter's Point, Queens, gets a 48-story skyscraper, the Citicorp Building, taller than any other in Queens or Brooklyn.

1989 "Only the little people pay taxes," real estate mogul Leona Helmsley tells an employee. She is sentenced to four years in prison for evading $1.2 million in federal taxes.

1989 The Central Park Jogger, a 29-year-old female investment banker, is beaten and raped by a group of black teenagers. A black teenage boy is murdered by a gang of whites in Bensonhurst, Brooklyn.

1989 Recycling is now mandatory in all five boroughs. Flyers with instructions are written in eight languages.

1989 Compressed natural gas burns clean and fuels a few—and little by little thousands—of the City's official vehicles.

1989 "How'm I doing?" After three terms, popular Mayor Ed Koch is felled by the City's financial state, the scandal at the Parking Violations Bureau, and continuing racial problems. He loses the Democratic primary to David Dinkins.

1990 David Dinkins is the City's first black mayor. Dinkins gives the melting pot a new label: gorgeous mosaic.

1990 A black boycott of two Korean produce markets on Church Street in Brooklyn is long and bitter, revealing tensions between two hard-pressed groups of New Yorkers.

1990 "Law and Order" begins filming on City streets and is a trendsetter. By 1995 New York is second only to Los Angeles as a venue for television production, with eleven prime-time and other shows set in the City. Producers spend about a billion dollars here a year, which generates about $2.3 billion in additional spending. (See 1998)

1990 Most subway cars are now air-conditioned.

1990 The high-stakes junk bond market collapses, and Drexel Burnham Lambert goes bankrupt. New Yorkers learn more than they ever wanted to know about insider trading from Ivan Boesky and Michael Milken.

1990 The art market crashes.

1990   Happy Land is one of the City's many unlicensed, inexpensive social clubs; 87 people, mostly Hondurans, die when a man quarrels with a female companion and sets the Bronx club on fire. The City shuts down 505 social clubs.

1990   Ellis Island opens as a museum nearly one hundred years after its debut as the country's immigration station. Computerized records enable visitors to look up their family names. Exhibits display objects from those tumultuous times, such as embroidered linens, children's toys, suitcases, journals.

1990   Brooklyn charges that the Board of Estimate, the City's governing body, is unfair. With nearly two million more people, Brooklyn has the same two votes as Staten Island. The U.S. Supreme Court agrees, and the Board of Estimate is disbanded.

1991   More than three centuries after Muslims most likely arrived among the Africans brought here as slaves, the first building designed as a mosque is built. Complete with minaret, the Islamic Cultural Center at 96th Street and Third Avenue is financed mostly by Kuwaitis and costs $17 million. The architect is the firm of Skidmore, Owings and Merrill.

1991   Guillermo Linares becomes a City Councilman and the first Dominican elected to public office in the United States.

From 1990 to 1994, 563,000 immigrants settle in the City from the Dominican Republic and its neighbors, and from Asia, Europe, Africa, and the former Soviet Union. The annual number of arrivals is 32 percent higher than the record-breaking 1980s.

Puerto Ricans and blacks born in the U.S., who made up the largest group moving to the post-war City, are leaving New York. By 1996 about 40 percent of the City's blacks are immigrants or children of immigrants from the Caribbean and elsewhere.

27,500 Native Americans live in Brooklyn and Queens, and comprise one of the fastest-growing minority groups in New York.

Mayor David Dinkins

1991   The African Burial Ground, dating back 300 years, is uncovered by construction workers near Foley Square. It is estimated that 20,000 people were buried in the five-acre site. Of the remains removed for study by Howard University anthropologists, about half are children. The Burial Ground and the Commons Historic District, including City Hall Park, are landmarked in 1993.

1991   A black child is accidentally killed by a Lubavitcher Hasid driver in Crown Heights. In the three-day race riot that erupts, a visiting Australian Jew is set upon and killed. His attacker is acquitted of the

Islamic Cultural Center

1992 In-line skates (rollerblades) create a new pastime and the City begins keeping statistics on accidents.

1992 Poetry in Motion feeds the straphanger's soul. Five million people a day see the short poems displayed like treasures in thousands of subway cars and buses.

1992 Reporters at NY 1, the all-New York City cable news channel, are required to live in the borough they cover.

1992 Bryant Park, behind the main branch of the New York Public Library, is transformed into a popular public space with cafés and movable chairs, so that office workers can get sunshine and cappuccino at lunchtime and meet friends for dinner after work. The drug dealers have been chased out.

College applicants want to spend their college years in New York. They like the glitter, the jobs, and the networking as well as having a place to explore. In the next five years applications to New York City colleges and universities will rise dramatically.

fatal stabbing, but in the 1997 civil trial, he is convicted. The following year the man who egged on the crowd is convicted and sentenced to 21 years in prison.

1992 New York has more cases of multi-drug-resistant tuberculosis than the rest of the country combined, but four years later, because of an initiative to give out hamburgers and other food incentives to patients taking nine pills a day, the disease shows a 46 percent decline.

1993 *The Golden Venture*, a freighter carrying 286 Chinese people with no papers but desperate to come to the United States, runs aground off the Rockaway peninsula in Queens. The ship is operated by the Fujianese mafia.

1993 Barnes & Noble opens its flagship superstore on Broadway and 82nd Street, with a café and armchairs. The discount chain knocks out independent booksellers, but it is said around town that it revives an interest in reading.

1993 Terrorists set off a bomb in an underground garage at the World Trade Center. Six die. New Yorkers are shaken by a renewed sense of vulnerability. One of the terrorists is apprehended when he returns to a rental office to get back his deposit on his "stolen" van. By 1998 seven conspirators are convicted. (But see page 138.)

1993 Staten Island votes in favor of secession from New York City. Among other grievances, it has lost some of its power in City government. The situation is still unresolved today.

1993 Red-tailed hawks begin to nest and breed on a Fifth Avenue high-rise overlooking Central Park.

1993 Riverbank State Park opens on twenty-eight landscaped acres atop a sewage treatment plant in Harlem. The state park has superb sports facilities and graceful promenades. It is one of Franz Leichter's many achievements in his thirty years in the state legislature.

1993 In the past four years, the City has lost 400,000 jobs and has seen welfare rise by 350,000 to 1.2 million recipients.

1993 An effective way of fighting gang violence is for the City to try gang members under the federal racketeering laws. It's a major breakthrough. In 1997 the Latin Kings' leader is sentenced to solitary confinement for life.

Bryant Park at lunchtime

Riverbank State Park

1994 Low-flow toilets—1.6 gallons—begin to replace the spectacular 3.5-gallon flush.

1994 The Parks Department is back in the business of buying land and is acquiring small parcels throughout the City.

1994 Harlem street vendors are cleared off 125th Street and moved to an improvised market on 116th Street and Lenox Avenue, but the crowds of shoppers don't come to this part of Harlem. 125th Street suffers a decline as well.

> Central Park, along with Yosemite and the Everglades, is listed as one of the top fourteen sites for bird-watching in the U.S. by *Travel & Leisure* magazine.

1994 The City mourns the death of Jacqueline Kennedy Onassis, one of its most beloved and admired residents.

1994 The magnificent old U.S. Custom House on Bowling Green reopens, after a $60 million renovation, to house the Smithsonian's National Museum of the American Indian. New York City fought successfully to save the building and to keep the museum from leaving the state. Visitors are welcomed at the entrance by crafted metal, stone, and enamel panels that recount in words and pictures the Indian story of these New York City islands.

1994 Seventeen snowstorms hit the City this winter, ice-cutters are busy on the Hudson, and the City efficiently fills 184,000 potholes.

1994 Tourists rediscover New York: 28 million people visit this year. The yearly tally will soon grow to over 33 million.

1994 Rudolph W. Giuliani, former prosecutor, wins the mayoral election on his second try and is the first Republican mayor in twenty-eight years. He immediately ignores party lines on some issues.

1995 Pope John Paul II celebrates mass in Central Park; 125,000 hear his salute to "great, great New York" and his call for generosity to the needy.

1995 The City, following the national trend, sets new rules for welfare, like fingerprinting recipients to prevent fraud, and mandatory work requirements. The working poor compete for job openings as well as places in day care for their children.

1995 The mayor slashes budgets to cut the City's debt. One agency, the Department of Parks, sells use of the parks to huge corporations, such as Disney.

1995 The young dance to loud racing techno music.

1995 Silicon Alley, made up of hundreds of start-up businesses, brings the media technology boom into New York City. By 1998, in the Flatiron District and SoHo, and from 34th to Canal Street, this growth industry is on a roller-coaster ride with venture capital, Wall Street investments, writer and artist talent, and over a hundred thousand employees.

1996 The Board of Education is one of the nation's largest consumers of anthracite coal and uses it to heat more than 250 of the City's schools, even though coal furnaces have long been banned in most City workplaces. In 1998, the Dickensian furnaces remain, and a boiler fireman still hand-shovels three tons of coal each day to feed the furnace.

1996 Judith S. Kaye, Chief Justice of the State of New York, reforms the way jury duty is handled. No more exemptions. Everyone must serve, but because of the expanded pool of jurors, the time required is reduced.

&

The two-martini lunch is a thing of the past. Lunch on the run or at the desk saves time and cuts calories. Bottled water goes along.

&

ATM machines, fax machines, E-mail, and the Web speed everything up but isolate the users of the latest electronic tools and put pressure on everyone to do things even faster than before. New York bike messengers lose a lot of business.

1996 The narrowest house in the City is 9 1/2 feet wide, built on Bedford Street around 1850. This year it can be rented for $6,000 a month. Among its past occupants were Edna St. Vincent Millay, Margaret Mead, and William Steig.

&

"My candle burns at both ends; it will not last the night; but ah, my foes, and oh, my friends—it gives a lovely light!" writes poet Edna St. Vincent Millay.

The narrowest house

1996 New Yorker Eleanor Roosevelt is remembered as "First Lady of the World" when a statue by Penelope Jencks is dedicated at Riverside Drive and 72nd Street.

Eleanor Roosevelt by Penelope Jencks

1996 After thirty years the lower Hudson River can support life again—for instance, one to two million striped bass. The river is so clean that marine borers and mollusks thrive and are eating away at barriers between river and island at Battery Park City. The upper Hudson, though, is second on a list of the nation's endangered rivers due to PCB contamination.

1996 Harlem Meer at 110th Street in Central Park is no longer a sludgy pond. It is cleaned up and now has swans, fishing poles for rent, and serene vistas.

1996 For the first time in Little League history, a championship game is held in the City (at Battery Park). Staten Island's South Shore team wins.

1996 The Board of Education dumped 100 unused school buildings in the fiscal crisis of the 1970s, so this year's overflow of 91,000 children has to study in hallways and closets.

1996 The Yankees make it to the World Series for the first time since 1981 and win it for the twenty-third time. "Take Me Out to the Ball Game" is sung in Spanish and English at the ticker-tape parade. The Bronx is looking good.

1996 The $100 million Science, Industry and Business Library, a branch of the New York Public Library, opens in the B. Altman building on Fifth Avenue and 34th Street. The famous old department store closed in 1990.

1996 There's more snow than the City has ever had since it started keeping records in 1869: 66.3 inches!

1996 For the first time since 1968, fewer than one thousand homicides are committed in the City. Murders by strangers are down to 19 percent of the total. Crime is down in many American cities.

West 95th Street

1996   Wall Street's profits soar to record highs. Bonuses soar, too, and fifteen hundred securities people each make over a million dollars this year. City tax revenues rise.

1996   The City's housing crisis is getting worse. Many immigrants have to live in subdivided basements in squalor reminiscent of tenement conditions at the turn of the century.

1996   The Board of Education, which was centralized in 1902 and decentralized in 1970, is now mostly centralized again. The Schools Chancellor, Rudy Crew, amasses power to improve the public schools.

1996   A John Street office building is converted into apartments. Tax incentives help landlords with these conversions. People are moving back into a downtown area that has been commercial for 200 years.

Times Square gets a boost from the Disney Corporation and its bottomless funds. The down-and-out crossroads of the world is being cleaned up and given a new identity. Theaters are being gutted and rebuilt, new hotels, businesses, and restaurants are opening.

1996   Municipal Radio Station WNYC, 820 AM and 93.9 FM, is bought from the City after seventy-four years. The independent classical music and news station is now owned by the WNYC Foundation, which is supported largely by listeners' contributions.

1996   Old Jeff, the 135-year-old bell, rings out again from the Jefferson Market Courthouse tower at Tenth Street and Sixth Avenue. The Victorian Gothic building itself, a stately relic from the Tweed era, was saved from the auction block in 1960 and adopted as a branch of the New York Public Library.

Retired people are turning their backs on the suburbs and moving to the walkable City for culture and company.

Jefferson Market Courthouse with 6th Avenue el, 1935, by Berenice Abbott

1997 Over 60,000 New Yorkers have died in the AIDS epidemic. Improved care and medication bring results; this year deaths from AIDS drop 48 percent. In 1998 GMHC opens the David Geffen Center for those suffering from the disease.

1997 Eight thousand dozen eggs and three boxcars of butter a week are sold by the last major butter-and-egg man in what was once Washington Market, now Tribeca.

1997 A new theater company, the Melting Pot, opens to bring performances about all kinds of people to audiences of all ages.

1997 A lower Manhattan sewage treatment plant intends, for maintenance purposes, to empty its holding tanks of 456 million gallons of raw sewage. A quarter of the daily total for the City, the sewage would run into the East River over four days. At the last minute the action is halted for environmental reasons.

1997 Metrocards and tokens can now be used at all 469 subway stations and on buses. Magnetic strip cards make free bus/ subway transfers possible for the first time, and soon unlimited monthly passes cut prices further. The riders get a break, and ridership increases dramatically.

The Mob is exploring new fields for white-collar crime, like health insurance and finance.

1997 "Your vote has been soaked in the blood of martyrs! How can you take that vote and sell it to somebody who won't stand up for you!" says Minister Al Sharpton, running for mayor.

1997 Incumbent Rudy Giuliani and Manhattan Borough President Ruth Messinger also fervently desire to be the City's next mayor. Messinger has come to politics via the school board, and asks what kind of a city cuts $6 billion from its public schools.

1997 State Majority Leader Joseph L. Bruno goes after rent regulations in force since World War II and 2.5 million renters are outraged. Speaker of the Assembly Sheldon Silver holds firm and tenants win a six-year extension. New York landlords have contributed $2 million to state Republican leaders over the last five years.

1997 Only 3 percent of all freight (from potatoes to nail polish) comes into New York City by rail. The rest comes in by truck, which snarls traffic, wrecks the roads, and fouls the air. Truck dependency "artificially inflates the cost of every grapefruit you buy," says U.S. Representative Jerrold Nadler, and the Automobile Association of America joins the push for rail freight.

1997 Newsstand operators, down to only 330 Citywide, mostly Indian, Pakistani, and Bangladeshi, count on pedestrians and busy intersections for their business. This year they face a ten-fold increase in licensing fees.

Oases of green planted by community gardeners a decade or two ago are uprooted and built on, though some construction companies, which have failed to heed the gardeners' warnings of underground streams, find their new buildings cracking and water in the basements.

1997 Over two hundred films are shot in the City this year, bringing in more than $5 billion and 75,000 jobs and setting a new record for Hollywood on Hudson. It is the City's fastest growing job sector.

1997 St. George, Staten Island, is planning a $100 million ferry terminal, which will also house the Staten Island Institute of Art and Sciences.

1997 Jazz moves back uptown. Old, new, and renovated clubs in Harlem are drawing musicians and audiences back into this cradle of jazz.

1997 Civic groups find that their handshake agreement on the Riverside South project on Manhattan's West Side is ignored and that the sliver park promised by Trump may have been scrapped, but the buildings will go up and residents fear desperate overcrowding of their neighborhood.

Newsstand

1997   March 17. The Great Hunger, the Irish potato famine of the 1840s, and its million dead, are remembered 150 years later in a minute of silence during the St. Patrick's Day parade.

1997   Beat poet and activist Allen Ginsberg, icon of the East Village, dies.

1997   The journalist Murray Kempton dies, a veteran of 10,000 columns about local New York.

1997   The Mayor has laid off 20,000 municipal employees and much of their work is soon being done by a low-paid labor force of workfare participants. The corrupt leaders of the municipal workers union, District 37, do not complain.

1997   March 23. Full moon, vernal equinox, clear skies. An almost total eclipse of the moon is observed, Mars is visible, and the Hale-Bopp comet can be seen shortly after sunset.

1997   The Community Service Society reports that 21 percent of the City—that's 1.5 million New Yorkers—are living in extreme poverty. Every day 2,600 people are turned away from soup kitchens in the City. (See 1998)

1997   New York State and New Jersey agree on a twenty-year plan to clean up pollutants in New York Harbor and the rivers that empty into it: the Hudson, Hackensack, Passaic, and Raritan.

1997   A watershed pact is designed to protect New York City's water supply at the source, 2,000 square miles of the Catskills, Westchester and Putnam Counties, but nevertheless, developers soon move in on the watershed.

1997   A Haitian immigrant, Abner Louima, is tortured at the 70th Precinct after he is picked up outside a nightclub on Flatbush

Avenue. The City is outraged. A plan to confront the blue wall of silence is made, but quickly dropped.

1997   The Mets play the Yankees. For the very first time, New York teams from the American League and the National League play each other in regular season games. New Yorkers get there by subway, and Yankee Stadium is packed.

1997   The number of child and adult baseball players has doubled in a decade, and soccer is also growing by leaps and bounds. The Parks Department issues half a million permits a year for games and practices in the five boroughs, but is having trouble meeting the demand for turf.

1997   In November *The Lion King*, produced by Disney, opens at the grand old New Amsterdam Theater, gloriously renovated, where Ziegfeld's *Follies* played.

1997   The month of Ramadan, commemorating the Koran, is recognized by the City's public school system on behalf of Muslim students. There are 500,000 Muslims in the City. They are a diverse group from all over the world, places like Eastern Europe, Egypt, the Philippines, and Guyana, and with varying levels of observance.

1997   The Harris Survey finds that New York is the city most Americans would like to live in.

1997   A teenager at Hunter College High School invents an electrochemical paintbrush that prints fifty words within the width of a human hair. He wins first prize in the Westinghouse Science Talent Search

The Lion King at the New Amsterdam Theater

(now Intel). Of the top ten high schools winning Westinghouse awards since 1942, nine are in New York City.

1997   Nuns at Sunset Park Family Life Center work to place foster children near their families and schools so that they are not wrenched from familiar surroundings. The City has more than 42,000 foster children.

❧

New York's new immigrants discuss their news and lives in over thirty languages, in 143 newspapers and magazines and on 22 cable channels and twelve radio stations.

1997   Mayor Giuliani installs the first sidewalk barriers to stop pedestrians crossing at certain intersections on Fifth and Sixth Avenues. Irate residents try their best to get jaywalking tickets but the police are slow to co-operate.

1998   A New York University study confirms the value of the City's small alternative high schools. With their more personalized settings, these schools have a better graduation rate than high schools with 2,000 or more students. The cost per graduate is virtually the same.

1998   Birds flock to a cleaner New York Harbor: herons, egrets, and ibis nest here, as well as 960 pairs of breeding cormorants, a bird new to these waters.

1998   Bella Abzug dies. The Democratic Congresswoman and feminist, known for her big hats and big heart, fought fiercely on behalf of peace in Vietnam, victims of breast cancer, and independence for New York City.

1998   The 3,700 ton Empire Theatre is sliced off its foundations and moved along soapy rails to its new home 170 feet west along 42nd Street. The cost is $588 per inch. The old playhouse will serve as the lobby for a new movie megaplex.

1998   NBC's Jerry Seinfeld gives 30 million viewers a week a New York City that is addictively inane and feels like home. Last show of an eight-year run: May 14.

❧

Queens has the greatest number of nationalities of any county in the U.S.

1998 The Board of Higher Education is seeking to cut back CUNY admissions drastically to students requiring remedial courses. Trustees say this is to raise standards. Critics see an attempt to privatize remedial instruction and put it beyond the means of low income students, effectively shutting them out.

1998 The hundredth anniversary of New York City's Consolidation of the five boroughs is celebrated.

1998 In Queens, the idiosyncratic and spacious Socrates Sculpture Park is saved for the public; and another inventive park, Gantry Plaza State Park, opens with a fog fountain, promenades, and piers.

1998 In Brooklyn, the famous Ravine in Prospect Park is being restored to the grandeur of Olmstead and Vaux's vision.

And the community is fighting to keep the nine-acre Empire Fulton State Park from going to a commercial developer. New York State bought the park in 1979 as "a future green haven from the city's pressures." The land nestles under the Brooklyn and Manhattan Bridges and has a glorious view of the harbor and skyline.

1998 The City breathes a sigh of relief as stock market money floods in and budgets show a surplus. Messes can be cleaned up and buildings planned. A sort of wealthy ease permeates the place, but can the good times survive a global financial crisis?

1998 The Danish *Regina Maersk*, one of the new superfreighters, steams into New York Harbor carrying a light cargo and nearly grazes the bottom. The harbor has to be deepened to remain the epicenter of east coast maritime commerce in the new millennium. The port generates $20 billion a year.

The Port of New York has needed a rail freight tunnel under the harbor for most of the century. Without the tunnel, ship cargo has to be transported by truck. A billion-dollar tunnel would link Brooklyn, through Bayonne, to the mainland. Politicians speak out for the port and the tunnel.

1998 The sky is falling. Collapsing scaffolding near Times Square kills one woman and closes streets for weeks. Loose bricks and other building parts have killed other residents this year. A new method of building inspection is overdue.

1998 Columbus Circle is about to lose the defunct Coliseum Convention Center and gain Columbus Centre, a huge residential/commercial complex that will give a permanent home to Jazz at Lincoln Center, and provide space for rehearsal rooms and television studios.

A Seinfeld *hangout*

1998 The City's 1.2 million Medicaid recipients are being switched to managed care, and will each have to select a plan. The goal is to move ordinary care out of the emergency room, provide preventive medicine, and save money. It will take a major initiative to train the City's neediest residents to be savvy medical consumers.

1998 A lone kayaker circumnavigates Manhattan Island at night, five hundred years after the Indians traveled the waterways.

1998 Garbage! Fresh Kills Landfill on Staten Island is full to overflowing, with trash piled as high as a seventeen-story building. It will close by 2002. Ocean dumping, incinerators, and local landfills have all been ruled out. The City must find a destination for 13,000 tons of residential trash a day, but other states don't want it, even for a fee.

1998 *The Amsterdam News*, New York's oldest continuously published black newspaper, founded in 1909, is taken over by its owner's daughter, Elinor R. Tatum, who will try to increase circulation among the metropolitan area's 2 million blacks.

1998 A New York City consortium of 25 leading medical schools, hospitals, and academic institutes is launching a 20-year study of 300,000 City residents of a variety of ethnic backgrounds to study causes of cancer and improve early detection and treatment. The study will re-establish New York as a leading biomedical research center.

1998 The Arthur Ashe Flushing Meadows Tennis Stadium opens. The stadium's 25-year lease with the City requires flights to and from La Guardia Airport to be rerouted during Tennis Open matches.

1998 The Mayor's tough welfare policy is aimed at making poor people self-reliant, but when the City purposely delays giving out applications for two other programs, food stamps and Medicaid, it undermines people's efforts to make it on their own, says the federal government.

1998 The Oak Point Link opens. This freight railroad shortcut through the Bronx, twenty years in the building, means freight trains no longer have to share commuter tracks on the "zig zag route" into the City.

1998 Demands at the City's 1,200 soup kitchens and pantries have increased 24 percent in one month. Many of the hungry are working poor trying to make ends meet on the $5.15-an-hour minimum wage.

1998 One Checker cab remains on City streets, down from a fleet of 5,000. The cherished and roomy Checker cab ride is now only a memory.

1998 Ellis Island, run by the National Park Service, is divided between New York and New Jersey, with most of it going to New Jersey. New York will keep the historic main hall.

1998 The first 13.5-mile segment of water tunnel No. 3 opens, and water flows from a Yonkers reservoir into City homes. The nation's largest public works project goes on underground, unbeknownst to most City residents.

1998 The New York Stock Exchange, after talk of moving out of town, agrees to stay in the financial district, thanks to subsidies and tax waivers of about $900 million.

1998 Washington Heights, with its 150,000 Dominicans, is gripped with excitement as Dominican-born Sammy Sosa battles Mark McGwire for the homerun record. Almost 10 percent of major league ball players are Dominican.

1998 The Bronx Bombers win their 24th World Series, this one against the San Diego Padres, in four straight games, their first sweep since 1950. New York City welcomes the Yankees home with a ticker-tape parade up the Canyon of Heroes. Politicians speak out for keeping the stadium in the Bronx rather than moving it to the west side of Manhattan or the Meadowlands in New Jersey.

1998 A new rail concourse for Pennsylvania Station is planned in the 1914 main post office building across Eighth Avenue. The 1960s demolition of Pennsylvania Station still haunts New Yorkers. Only in New York is there a second great building to make up for the mistake of tearing down the first.

1998 Grand Central Terminal proudly celebrates its 85th anniversary with a $200 million renovation which includes a set of marble staircases to balance the original ones, and new chandeliers. A sea-green sky, its constellations outfitted with new fiber optic stars, has been cleaned of decades of nicotine and pollution. A tiny patch of dirt is left

Grand Central Terminal

untouched in the northwest corner to show how filthy the ceiling was. For the half million people who pass through Grand Central each day, the newly gorgeous terminal symbolizes the importance of public spaces, and allows New York to celebrate an exhilarating recovery from the long-hobbling second-class status of the railroad.

1998 The biggest subway system in the world is nominated for the National Register of Historic Places, a move that acknowledges the subway's great role in the history and growth of New York City.

1998 Highbridge in the west Bronx is gaining a small park, designed and built by teenagers who attend the Liberty Partnership program at the School of Visual Arts. Their "meditative park" is a quiet place away from the stresses of neighborhood life.

1998 In another bid to escape harsh realities of City life a dozen teenagers in the Bronx are building a 14-foot wooden rowboat, a Whitehall, dating from the 1800s when the boat was used as a ferry on the City's waterways. Vassar graduate Adam Green starts an after-school workshop in a basement for neighborhood kids.

1998 The number of homicides in the City drops to 629, below the 1964 total.

1998 How in the world will computers know that 00 means the year 2000 and not 1900 all over again? The glitch is known as Y2K. The City's 687 computer systems are being updated for practice runs in 1999.

Room 315, New York Public Library, after renovation

&

Residents with a glazed look in their eyes are probably talking on their cell phones. These ubiquitous gadgets impose just one side of conversations on commuters, who might prefer quiet, as well as on diners and shoppers.

1998   The vast and ornate main reading room at the 42nd Street branch of the New York Public Library opens after a $15 million renovation which includes installation of computers. Renamed the Rose Reading Room for Frederick P. Rose and Sandra Priest Rose who funded the refurbishment, this beautiful and grand space is once again a fit place for the acquisition and dispensation of knowledge. Go and admire Room 315 for yourself.

The steel drum, Trinidad's national instrument, is happily moving into some public school music programs in the City, bringing the sound of the Caribbean into youngsters' lives.

1998   To put the City into safe working order—especially subways and schools—will require $40 billion more than the $52 billion now planned for, says Comptroller Alan Hevesi. Deferred maintenance will only drive up costs. Hevesi's report is the first in twenty years to bring engineers and investigators together to estimate the City's pressing needs.

1998   The majority of New Yorkers say that life in New York City is better than it was four years ago.

The City of neighborhoods offers parents an old-fashioned way to bring up their children, with local schools, community spirit, and a sense of the wide world. New York City, on the edge of the continent, races toward the millennium, anticipating a huge celebration. This great City holds out the promise of America through its diverse neighborhoods, its energy, and its resilience, and vows to carry into the new era the spirit and tolerance that have always set it apart.

On Tuesday, September 11, 2001, in a terrorist attack, two hijacked passenger jets destroy the Twin Towers and the five other buildings of the World Trade Center. The crash and collapse of the Towers kill around 2,800 working people from all over the world and the United States, including 343 firefighters, 78 other uniformed rescuers, and civilian heroes of all kinds. The Towers stand long enough for thousands to get out. A third plane attacks the Pentagon. Passengers in a fourth hijacked plane learn of the attacks and thwart the terrorists; the plane crashes in rural Pennsylvania.

ACKNOWLEDGMENTS

For a short book, there is a long list of people who have helped and encouraged us. Thanks to Peter Simmons, Deputy Director for Exhibitions, Publications and Electronic Media at the Museum of the City of New York, and Eileen Kennedy Morales, Manager of Collections Access for the Museum; to designer Omega Clay; to Loomis Mayer and Jacky Philpotts at Fordham University Press; to agent Charlotte Sheedy; to Philip Mattera at the National Writers Union; to Helene Silver at City & Company; to historians and writers Rickie Solinger, Gerald Markowitz, David C. Hammack, Carol Groneman, Norman J. Brouwer, and Rudy Gray; to anthropologists Robert S. Grumet, John Kraft and Anne Buddenhagen; to Daniel Morgenroth and Janet Chalmers and to researcher Isaac Esterman; to Toni Levi, Phyllis Kantar, Joyce Morgenroth, Laura Harrington, and Sharon Zane for their editorial eye; to Saundra Dancy and Dee Dee Aikens at the Lloyd George Sealy Library, John Jay College, CUNY; to librarians Marion Weston at the Fashion Institute of Technology and Betty Odabashian at the Schomburg Center for Research in Black Culture, and to librarian Rebeline Landsman. All these people and many more have helped to hallow and celebrate this city.

Quotation Sources

ALLEN, OLIVER E.
New York, New York, 1990

BROWN, CLAUDE
Manchild in the Promised Land, 1965

DENTON, DANIEL
"A Brief Description of New York," 1670 in
Jaray, ed., *Historic Chronicles of New Amsterdam,
Colonial New York and Early Long Island,* Series
Two, 1968

GLUECK, GRACE, AND PAUL GARDNER
Brooklyn: People and Places, Past and Present,
1991

GOLDBERGER, PAUL
*The City Observed: New York, A Guide to the Archi-
tecture of Manhattan,* 1979

GRUMET, ROBERT S.
Lenapes, 1986

HAMMACK, DAVID C.
*Power and Society: Greater New York at the Turn of
the Century,* 1982

HOWE, IRVING
World of Our Fathers, 1976

JACKSON, KENNETH T.
"Prison ships," in Jackson, ed., *The Encyclopedia of New York City,* 1995

JOHNSON, JAMES WELDON
Black Manhattan, 1930

KENNEY, ALICE P.
Stubborn for Liberty: The Dutch in New York, 1975

KLEIN, MILTON M.
"Introduction," in Klein, ed., *New York: The
Centennial Years 1676–1976,* 1976

LANKEVICH, GEORGE J.,
AND HOWARD B. FURER
A Brief History of New York City, 1984

MACKAY, DONALD A.
The Building of Manhattan, 1987

PYE, MICHAEL
Maximum City: The Biography of New York, 1991

RINK, OLIVER A.
*Holland on the Hudson: An Economic and Social
History of Dutch New York,* 1986

SANTE, LUC
Low Life: Lures and Snares of Old New York, 1991

SANTE, LUC
"The Possessed," *The New York Review of
Books,* July 16, 1992

SHRECKER, ELLEN W.
"McCarthyism," in Jackson, ed., *The Encyclopedia of New York City,* 1995

SILVER, NATHAN
Lost New York, 1967

STANSELL, CHRISTINE
*City of Women: Sex and Class in New York,
1789–1860,* 1986

STEINBECK, JOHN
"Autobiography: Making of a New Yorker,"
The New York Times Magazine, February 1, 1953

STOKES, I. N. PHELPS
New York Past and Present, 1939

TRAGER, JAMES
The People's Chronology, 1994

VAN DER DONCK, ADRIAEN
A Description of the New Netherlands, 1655

WHITE, E. B.
"New York in March," *The New Yorker*, March 2, 1935

BIBLIOGRAPHY

Allen, Oliver E. *New York, New York: A History of the World's Most Exhilarating and Challenging City.* New York: Atheneum, 1990.

Axelrod, Alan, and Charles Phillips. *What Every American Should Know About American History.* Holbrook, Mass.: Bob Adams, 1992.

Bayor, Ronald H., and Timothy J. Meagher, eds. *The New York Irish.* Baltimore: The John Hopkins University Press, 1996.

Bergreen, Laurance. *As Thousands Cheer: The Life of Irving Berlin.* New York: Viking Penguin, 1990.

Berlin, Ira. *Many Thousands Gone: The First Two Centuries of Slavery in North America.* Cambridge, Mass: Harvard University Press, 1998.

Bolton, R. P. *New York City in Indian Possession.* New York: Museum of the American Indian, Gustav Heye Foundation, 1975.

Brown, Claude. *Manchild in the Promised Land.* New York: Signet, NAL, 1965.

Burrows, Edwin G., and Mike Wallace. *Gotham: A History of New York City to 1898.* New York: Oxford University Press, 1999.

Cook, Blanche Wiesen. *Eleanor Roosevelt, Vol. I: 1884–1933.* New York: Penguin, 1992.

Countryman, Edward. *A People in Revolution: The American Revolution and Political Society in New York, 1760–1790.* Baltimore: Johns Hopkins University Press, 1981.

Ellis, Edward Robb. *The Epic of New York City: A Narrative History.* New York: Old Town Books, 1990.

Foner, Nancy, ed. *New Immigrants in New York.* New York: Columbia University Press, 1987.

Frommer, Harvey. *New York City Baseball: The Last Golden Age, 1947–1957.* New York: Macmillan, 1980.

Glueck, Grace, and Paul Gardner. *Brooklyn: People and Places, Past and Present.* New York: Abrams, 1991.

Goldberger, Paul. *The City Observed: New York, A Guide to the Architecture of Manhattan.* New York: Vintage Books, 1979.

Goodfriend, Joyce D. *Before the Melting Pot: Society and Culture in Colonial New York City, 1664–1730.* Princeton, N J: Princeton University Press, 1992.

Grumet, Robert S. *Native American Place Names in New York City.* New York: Museum of the City of New York, 1981.

———. *Lenapes.* New York: Chelsea, 1986.

Hammack, David C. *Power and Society: Greater New York at the Turn of the Century.* New York: Russell Sage Foundation, 1982.

Homberger, Eric. *The Historical Atlas of New York City: A Visual Celebration of Nearly 400 Years of New York City's History.* New York: Henry Holt, 1994.

Howe, Irving. *World of our Fathers: The Journey of the East European Jews to America and the Life They Found and Made.* New York: Harcourt Brace Jovanovich, 1976.

Jackson, Kenneth T., ed. *The Encyclopedia of New York City.* New Haven: Yale University Press; New York: New-York Historical Society, 1995.

Jameson, J. F., ed. *Narratives of New Netherland, 1609–1664.* New York: Barnes & Noble, 1967.

Jaray, Cornell, ed. *Historic Chronicles of New Amsterdam, Colonial New York and Early Long Island.* 2 vols. Port Washington, N Y: Ira J. Friedman, 1968.

Johnson, James Weldon. *The Autobiography of an Ex-Colored Man.* New York: Dover Publications, Inc., 1995.

———. *Black Manhattan.* New York: Da Capo, 1930.

Kammen, Michael. *Colonial New York: A History.* Millwood, N Y: KTO Press, 1975.

Kasson, John F. *Amusing the Million: Coney Island at the Turn of the Century.* New York: Hill & Wang, 1978.

Kenney, Alice P. *Stubborn for Liberty: The Dutch in New York.* Syracuse, N Y: Syracuse University Press, 1975.

Kessner, Thomas, and Betty Boyd Caroli. *Today's Immigrants, Their Stories: A New Look at the Newest Americans.* Oxford: Oxford University Press, 1982.

Kieran, John. *A Natural History of New York City.* Boston: Houghton Mifflin, 1959; New York: Fordham University Press, 1982.

Klein, Milton M., ed. *New York: The Centennial Years, 1676–1976.* Port Washington, N Y: Kennikat, 1976.

Kouwenhoven, John A. *The Columbia Historical Portrait of New York: An Essay in Graphic History.* New York: Harper & Row, 1972.

Kraft, Herbert C. *The Lenape: Archaeology, History, and Ethnography.* Newark: New Jersey Historical Society, 1986.

Kraft, Herbert C., and John T. Kraft. *The Indians of Lenapehoking.* South Orange, N.J.: Seton Hall University Museum, 1975.

Lankevich, George J. *American Metropolis: A History of New York City.* New York: New York University Press, 1998.

Lankevich, George J., and Howard B. Furer. *A Brief History of New York City.* Port Washington, N Y: Associated Faculty Press, 1984.

Mackay, Donald A. *The Building of Manhattan: How Manhattan Was Built over Ground and Underground, from the Dutch Settlers to the Skyscraper.* New York: Harper & Row, 1987.

McKay, Ernest A. *The Civil War and New York City.* Syracuse, NY: Syracuse University Press, 1990.

Markowitz, Gerald E., and David Rosner. *Children, Race, and Power: Kenneth and Mamie Clark's Northside Center.* Charlottesville, Va.: University Press of Virginia, 1996.

Martin, Edward Winslow. *The Secrets of the Great City: A Work Descriptive of the Virtues and the Vices, the Mysteries, Miseries and Crimes of New York City.* Philadelphia: Jones Brothers, 1868.

Melville, Herman. *Moby-Dick, or The Whale.* 1851. New York: Signet, 1961.

Morison, Samuel Eliot. *The European Discovery of America.* 2 vols. New York: Oxford University Press, 1971–74.

Morris, Ira K. *Morris's Memorial History of Staten Island, New York.* 2 vols. New York: Memorial Publishing, 1898.

Morris, Lloyd. *Incredible New York: High Life and Low Life of the Last Hundred Years.* New York: Random House, 1951.

Moscow, Henry. *The Street Book.* New York: Fordham University Press, 1978.

———. *The Book of New York Firsts: Unusual, Arcane, and Fascinating Facts in the Life of New York City.* New York: Macmillan, 1982.

New York City Landmarks Preservation Commission. *African Burial Ground and the Commons Historic District.* Designation Report. 1993.

Newfield, Jack, and Wayne Barrett. *City for Sale: Ed Koch and the Betrayal of New York.* New York: Harper & Row, 1988.

Newfield, Jack, and Paul Du Brul. *The Abuse of Power: The Permanent Government and the Fall of New York.* New York: Viking, 1977.

Osofsky, Gilbert. *Harlem–The Making of a Ghetto: Negro New York, 1890–1930.* New York: Harper & Row, 1966.

Ottley, Roi, and William Weatherby, eds. *The Negro in New York: An Informal Social History.* New York: The New York Public Library, 1967.

Platt, Richard. *Smithsonian Visual Timeline of Inventions from the First Stone Tools to Satellites and Superconductors.* London: Dorling Kindersley, 1994.

Plunz, Richard. *A History of Housing in New York City: Dwelling Type and Social Change in the American Metropolis.* New York: Columbia University Press, 1990.

Pool, David De Sola. *Portraits Etched in Stone: Early Jewish Settlers, 1682–1831.* New York: Columbia University Press, 1952.

Pye, Michael. *Maximum City: The Biography of New York.* London: Sinclair- Stevenson, 1991.

Riis, Jacob A. Edited and with an introduction by David Leviatin. *How the Other Half Lives: Studies Among the Tenements of New York.* Boston: St. Martin's Press, 1996.

Rink, Oliver A. *Holland on the Hudson: An Economic and Social History of Dutch New York.* Ithaca, N Y: Cornell University Press, 1986.

Robertson-Lorant, Laurie. *Melville: A Biography.* New York: Clarkson Potter, 1996.

Rogasky, Barbara. *Smoke and Ashes: The Story of the Holocaust.* New York: Holiday House, 1988.

Rosenberg, Deena. *Fascinating Rhythm: The Collaboration of George and Ira Gershwin.* New York: Dutton, 1991.

Rosenzweig, Roy, and Elizabeth Blackmar. *The Park and the People: A History of Central Park.* Ithaca, N Y: Cornell University Press, 1992.

Rosner, David, ed. *Hives of Sickness: Public Health and Epidemics in New York City.* New Brunswick, N J: Museum of the City of New York and Rutgers University Press, 1995.

Ruttenber, E. M. *The History of Indian Tribes of Hudson's River, 1700–1850.* 1872. 2 vols. Facsimile reprint, Saugerties, N Y: Hope Farm, 1992.

Salwen, Peter. *Upper West Side Story: A History and Guide.* New York: Abbeville, 1989.

Sante, Luc. *Low Life: Lures and Snares of Old New York.* New York: Random House, 1991.

Silver, Nathan. *Lost New York.* Boston: Houghton Mifflin, 1967.

Sleeper, Jim. *The Closest of Strangers: Liberalism and the Politics of Race in New York.* New York: W.W. Norton, 1990.

Stansell, Christine. *City of Women: Sex and Class in New York 1789–1860.* Urbana: University of Illinois Press, 1986.

Still, Bayrd. *Mirror for Gotham: New York as Seen by Contemporaries from Dutch Days to the Present.* New York: New York University Press, 1956; New York: Fordham University Press, 1994.

Stokes, I. N. Phelps. *New York Past and Present, 1524–1939.* Published for the 1939 World's Fair.

Trager, James. *The People's Chronology.* Revised. New York: Henry Holt, 1994.

———. *The Women's Chronology.* New York, Henry Holt, 1994.

Ultan, Lloyd. *The Bronx in the Frontier Era: From the Beginning to 1696.* New York: Bronx County Historical Society, 1993.

Upton, Dell, ed. *America's Architectural Roots: Ethnic Groups that Built America.* New York: John Wiley & Sons, 1986.

Van der Donck, Adriaen. *A Description of the New Netherlands* [1655, trans. 1841]. Edited by Thomas F. O'Donnell. Syracuse, N Y: Syracuse University Press, 1968.

van der Zee, Henri, and Barbara van der Zee. *A Sweet and Alien Land: The Story of Dutch New York.* New York: Viking, 1978.

Weatherford, Jack. *Indian Givers: How the Indians of the Americas Transformed the World.* New York: Fawcett Columbine, 1988.

Wexler, Alice. *Emma Goldman: An Intimate Life.* New York: Pantheon, 1984.

Wilson, Sherrill D. *New York City's African Slaveowners: A Social and Material Culture History.* New York: Garland, 1994.

Works Progress Administration. *WPA Guide to New York City.* 1939. New York: Random House, 1992.

Wright, Carol von Pressentin. *Blue Guide New York.* New York: W.W. Norton, 1991.

Picture Credits

iii *The Narrows from Staten Island*, W. H. Bartlett, engraved by J. White for the Columbian Magazine

v *Seal of the Province of New Netherland*, 1623

v *Seal of the City of New Amsterdam*, 1654

vii *Seal of New York City*, 1915

vii *Current seal of New York City*, revised 1977

1 Turtle petroglyph, stone carving, image courtesy of The LuEsther T. Mertz Library of the New York Botanical Garden, Bronx, New York

2 *Manhattan Island Before the Dutch Settlement*

3 *Giovanni da Verrazano*, G. Locchi, del., F. Allegrini, inci., 1767

4 *Henry Hudson*, E. G. Williams & Bro., engravers

4 The Half-Moon, *Morris's Memorial History of Staten Island, New York*, 1898

5 Adraien Block's *Figurative Map of "Nieu Nederlandt,"* 1616

6 Flag of the West India Company, *Morris's Memorial History of Staten Island, New York*, 1898

7 *View of New Amsterdam*, Joost Hartgers, date depicted 1626–1628, published 1651

9 Detail from *Lawsuit Decided by Wouter Van Twiller*, H. R. Robinson, 1865

11 *The Prototype View of New Amsterdam*, 1650–1653

12 *Dance on the Battery in the Presence of Peter Stuyvesant*, Asher B. Durand, 1838

12 *Stadhuys, Coenties Slip*, 1652

13 *City Wall or Palisade on Wall Street*, 1662

14 *The White Hall, Governor Stuyvesant's City House*

14 *Heere Gracht (Broad Street)*, 1663

15 Redraft of *The Castello Plan*, by Jacques Cortelyou, 1660; redraft by John Wolcott Adams under the direction of I. N. Phelps Stokes

16 Deed granting land in Brooklyn to Thomas Lambertse, signed by Peter Stuyvesant and Cornelis van Ruyven, May 15, 1664

17 *Ancient View of the Present Junction of Pearl & Chatham Sts.*, lith. of Sarony, Major & Knapp for *D. T. Valentine's Manual*, 1861

18 Details from *A South Prospect of the Flourishing City of New York in the Province of New York in America*, engraved by William Burgis, 1717, published by Thomas Bakewell, 1747

19 Tombstone of Benjamin Bueno de Mesquita, 1683, courtesy of Congregation Shearith Israel

20–21 Detail and entire view of *A South Prospect of the Flourishing City of New York in the Province of New York in America*, engraved by William Burgis, 1717, published by Thomas Bakewell, 1747

22 *Brother Banvards*, John Banvard, 1776

INDEX

About the Authors

JANE MUSHABAC has written a book on Herman Melville. Her work has appeared in the *Village Voice* and other periodicals, and she has been a Harvard University fellow. She is a professor at New York City College of Technology, CUNY.

ANGELA WIGAN has written book reviews for *Time* magazine and other publications. She is a graduate of Columbia University's Oral History Program.